# The Secret Gospels

## A Harmony of Apocryphal Jesus Traditions

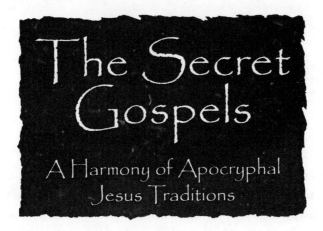

# The Secret Gospels

## A Harmony of Apocryphal Jesus Traditions

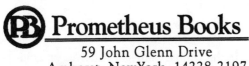

Edited and Translated by
## R. Joseph Hoffmann

 WESTMINSTER COLLEGE–OXFORD: CRITICAL STUDIES IN RELIGION

**Prometheus Books**
59 John Glenn Drive
Amherst, NewYork 14228-2197

Published 1996 by Prometheus Books

00 99 98 97 96     5 4 3 2 1

Library of Congress Cataloging-in-Publication Data

The secret Gospels : a harmony of Apocryphal Jesus traditions / edited and translated by R. Joseph Hoffmann.
    p.    cm.
Includes bibliographical references (p.   ).
ISBN 1–57392–069–X (cloth : alk. paper)
    1. Apocryphal Gospels—Harmonies. English. 2. Jesus Christ—Biography—Apocryphal and legendary literature. I. Hoffmann, R. Joseph.
BS850.A3H64    1996
229′.8052—dc20                    96–7938
                                        CIP

Printed in the United States of America on acid-free paper

To
Morton Smith
ut cum reverentia serviatur tibi
and to
Carolyn, Marthe, and Anna
in caritate perpetua dilexi vos

# Contents

7

# Preface

"This little babe so few days old is come to rifle Satan's fold.
All hell doth at his presence quake, tho' he himself for cold do shake:
Who in this dark unarm'd wise, the gates of hell he will surprise."
(Robert Southwell, *The Burning Babe*)

The New Testament provides two accounts of the birth of Jesus in the opening chapters of the Gospels of Matthew and Luke. It has long been recognized that the two accounts conflict in important ways: Luke, for example, thinks of Nazareth as the hometown of Mary and Joseph and he locates them in Bethlehem on the occasion of a census. Matthew regards Bethlehem as the hometown and places the family in Nazareth, after recounting a long sojourn in Egypt where they had fled to escape persecution by Herod and later by his son Archelaus. These and attendant differences in the accounts seem to suggest that the two evangelists were working from different traditions which incorporated different historical and legendary detail, even though, in important respects—the Davidic

9

descent of Jesus, the place of birth (Bethlehem), the chastity of Mary, and the miraculous events surrounding the birth of the redeemer—the accounts form a theological whole.

The early Christians were fond of such stories. In response to the demand of the faithful, some early writers, following the lead of Matthew and Luke, went on to provide even fuller narratives of the birth of Jesus and accounts of his family history. These accounts will not be familiar to many today, chiefly because their status in the official life of the church has been marginal and occasionally controversial. Nevertheless, from the early second century—or not long after the accounts in the canonical gospels were transcribed—a variety of stories began to appear, fueled by Christian piety, devotion, and simple curiosity.

The sources that have been used in compiling this book are thus very ancient. They come from all corners of the early Christian community—from Egypt and Syria, where literary activity flourished in Alexandria and Antioch, from Rome and its satellites in North Africa and Greece, and from early medieval Europe. Modern readers will be struck both by their literary crudeness as well as by what will look, measured even by the standards of the canonical gospels, theatrical and legendary.

Whatever our response to the literary decoration of the apocryphal infancy stories, however, their writers intended them to be supports for an enlarged *armoire* of Christian beliefs—in the virgin birth of Jesus, the holiness of Joseph, the miraculous powers of the infant Christ, and even the extraordinary stature of a young John the Baptist. Contemporary Christians may well do without tales of Anna's revenge on her persecutors, Elizabeth's being swallowed for safekeeping by a mountain of God, Jesus' contest with Egyptian dragons, or Virgin and son being ferried across the desert by a pillar of cloud. Our long acquaintance with the canonical sources has, to a degree, predisposed us to regard the apocryphal, or "hidden," traditions as evidence of the simplicity of the first age of Christian believers. This preference for canonical stories presupposes that the tales of God's supernatural dealings with the world as recorded in the Bible are somehow truer than the ones that were excluded from the canon, a view which many biblical scholars and historians today find, at best, a sentimental attachment to familiar myths. If the episodes above possess the incredible sound of the unfamiliar, the stories of Jesus feeding the five thousand (or four thousand), crossing the sea of Galilee on foot (a shallow lake it was, quipped the philosopher Porphyry), changing water to wine at his mother's behest, raising the dead, and casting out a legion of demons at Gadara hardly constitute a sober report against which to measure the accuracy of noncanonical texts. In the post-Christian era, it is not only the supernatural but the social construction of canons that comes under scrutiny. In the third century, when a majority of the apocryphal works were composed (though many are earlier), it was not a rude emphasis on the supernatural that caused their exclusion from the authorized indices of scripture. It was rather that the church had made up its collective mind about the miracles and magic of Jesus by drawing a fence around "approved readings," partly as a discouragement to heretics like the gnostics who had developed their own factories for the production of "Christian" gospels, partly to limit the continued popularization of the Jesus tradition with its ever increasing stock of tales and stories about the wonders performed by the god-man. It was once said by a German church historian that the theological problem for the church in the second century was not in getting people to believe that Jesus was God, but in convincing them that he was a man. The apocryphal or "secret" gospels shed considerable light on the seriousness of that problem.

There are thus good reasons for knowing these early Christian tales. They give us valuable insight into the devotional habits and thought-world of the early church, even glimpses of the development of important doctrines, such as the immaculate conception, the divinity of Jesus, and the assumption of the Virgin into heaven. Taken together, they are an odd mix of legend, morality tale, drama, and hagiography ("saints' lives"). Their authors are for the most part unknown, even though the most important of them were assigned from an early date to apostolic authors such as James "the Lord's brother" and the apostle Thomas.

I have brought these gospels together in a "harmony," that is, an artificial arrangement which seeks to reduce repetition while including important elements from a variety of apocryphal sources. Those who wish to know more about the background to these sources and my methods here will want to read the introduction, where the details of the project are set out in some detail. But there is no need to begin with the introduction. The apocryphal infancy tradition speaks for itself, and I would suggest that the best way to approach the subject—for those who have no prior acquaintance with these stories—is to begin with the works themselves: to read through from beginning to end, then to go back and read the introduction to the book. Along the way, questions will arise—about the sources and their origin, about details, even perhaps about the historical reliability of the apocryphal infancy tradition. Some of these questions I have tried to anticipate and to answer in the introduction and in the notes accompanying the text. A more scholarly treatment and an up-to-date bibliography may be found in J. K. Elliott's *The Apocryphal New Testament* (Oxford: Clarendon, 1993).

I think the reader will find, as I have always found, that these stories are compelling, curious, occasionally amusing, and a great deal besides. I offer this collection as a window onto a simpler time when the theological struggle to express belief in the divinity of Jesus was not confined to bishops in council but included the creative piety of the Christian faithful.

# Preface

\* \* \*

This project has been several years in the making. It began as an attempt to enlarge the Christmas story for my (then) three-year-old daughter, who, like children in every age, enjoyed stories about angels singing in high heaven and frightened shepherds wending their way to the Christ child's manger-bed. She also enjoyed stories from D'Aulaire's *Greek Myths* and wondered, by the age of five, whether there were any "other" stories about Jesus.

The answer, of course, is yes—but they're not for children. Or at least that would have been the church's answer. My own response, however, to a budding mythographer and humanist had to be yes—and you will notice in these stories that Jesus behaves like the mischievous young god Hermes.\* The apocryphal Christ child is a precocious divinity who causes trouble for his mother virtually from the moment he wriggles out of his wrappings. Like Hermes he is the son of the chief god, born in a cave. Like Hermes, he delights in deceiving his parents. And like Hermes, he enjoys displaying his power, and wins God's (Zeus') affection through trickery. That seemed to satisfy my daughter.

As a specialist in early Christian literature and the evolution of doctrine, I was struck by the fact that there are many beyond the age of five who do not know these stories: that when students first hear about them—if at all—at age eighteen or twenty in a college lecture course in literature or religion, they are offered up as the eccentric stories of the church's immaturity, something left on the cutting

---

\*"According to the earliest Hermes tradition, he was the son of Zeus and Maia and became a messenger of the gods. Cunning from birth, Hermes is told by his father to help in the making of Pandora and to put in her mind the shamelessness of a dog and the deceit of a thief." (Hesiod, *Theogony* 939; 65–70. ET, R. M. Frazer, *The Poems of Hesiod* (Norman, Okla.: University of Oklahoma Press, 1983).

room floor after the canonical life of Jesus had been slapped shut between vellum covers. Thus regarded, they are easy to ignore as the work of ancient unborn-again eccentrics who were out to damage God's word in scripture. But that opinion is both anachronistic and uninformed. In fact, the canonical texts have similar beginnings in oral traditions and devotional habits of the early Christian community. To put it more precisely, the difference between canonical and apocryphal traditions is not that the former are historical while the latter are legendary, but that the canonical tradition represents the authorized Jesus-legend of the church, while the apocryphal traditions remain unauthorized.

Although the apocryphal infancy stories have been pushed aside by the history and use of the church's official canon, they did not begin their life as marginal (nor in most cases as heretical) works. It does them a kind of belated justice, therefore, to free them from the "specialist's corpus" in which they have been confined for so many centuries.

I wish to thank the following for their contributions—general and specific—trusting that they will know why they have been named: Professor Thomas Wright of Auburn University; Professors George Williams and Krister Stendahl, *emeriti* of Harvard Divinity School; Professor Maurice Wiles of Oxford; Professor George Mendenhall of the University of Michigan; Professors Stephen Harris and Robert Platzner of California State University, Sacramento; Professor Gerald Larue of the University of Southern California; and my industrious colleagues in the School of Theology of Westminster College, Oxford, above all to Dr. Bernard Farr who is the guiding spirit for one of the most innovative programs in the study of Christianity in Europe. As ever, words of gratitude are due Professor Paul Kurtz, emeritus of the State University of New York at Buffalo, and to Steven Mitchell, the sagacious editor of Prometheus Books. Eugene

O'Connor has turned a classicist's eye on the whole work, and I am indebted to him for his masterful editing.

I refrain from thanking my wife, Carolyn Ruis Hoffmann, overmuch for her encouragement, or my "older" daughter for the wide-eyed fascination—my reward for being chief storyteller in this household—which helped me to conceive this project and to sustain my enthusiasm for it over the past several years.

# Introduction

# The Secret Gospels:
## A Harmony of Apocryphal Traditions

Interest in the so-called apocryphal literature of the Old and New Testaments has been encouraged in the last generation by the discovery of new resources and fresh translations of existing sources. During my own student days at Harvard Divinity School and later at Oxford, there was considerable excitement over the completion of work on the first serviceable translation of the Coptic-gnostic papyri from Nag Hammadi—the "gnostic gospels," so called because they had originated in a Christian cult which saw Jesus as a savior-revealer who imparted knowledge of salvation (*gnosis*) to a select number of believers. Thousands have now benefited from the light such discoveries have shed on the study of early Christianity and its surrounding culture. At the same time, the publication of the fragments from Khirbet Qumran (the Dead Sea Scrolls) has continued (at something less than an impressive pace perhaps) and a number of other scholarly "team efforts," notably those of the compilers of the pseudepigraphical writings of the Old Testament,[1] and the work of the Westar Project and the Context

Group have shown just how much early Christianity absorbed from the cultural eddies from which it finally emerged.[2]

These, as well as new developments in the study of biblical literature—computer-assisted analyses of biblical language, greater acceptance of the procedures of "secular" literary, sociological, and historical criticism, to name only the most significant—have made a permanent mark on our understanding of early Christian life, thought, and literature. In the late 1990s we know a great deal more about the way in which the New Testament was put together than did people in 1890, or in 1290. Our determination to rediscover the patterns of early Christian thought and expression and to situate the political evolution of the Christian church within the conflictive environment of the late Hellenistic world has paid impressive scholarly dividends.

With so much that is new and exciting, it is easy to be distracted from what we have known for a long time. What we have known is that the twenty-seven books of the New Testament represent only a fraction of the literature produced in the first five centuries of the Christian church. The canon, or list, of approved writings is really no more than the formalization of a consensus which existed prior to its ultimate expression in the fourth century[3]; the list itself is an admission that gospels, letters, acts, and apocalypses from various quarters had to be excluded or "marginalized."

Much of what was finally excluded was, in the doctrinal arena of its own time, "heretical"—a departure from the norm of the Church's teaching as propounded by important bishops and councils. The gnostic "gospels" surviving from Nag Hammadi are a case in point. Condemnation of the teachings they embody, and in some cases of particular works, can be traced to the middle decades of the second century C.E., a period when the New Testament canon itself was fluid. The so-called gnostics—thought by the bishop Irenaeus in somewhat exaggerated terms to have derived their notions from the arch-heretic Simon Magus (Acts 8)—are blamed for "mixing lime with the word of God [in scripture]."[4] But Irenaeus, despite his officially good intentions, was only partly right. The gnostics were strange birds by any reckoning, as an impartial reading of their sacred texts will suggest. But their strangeness was itself a spur to the "orthodox" bishops to state exactly what in scripture and teaching was *less* than strange. Heresy and heretics gave Christian intellectuals an opportunity to define the standards (*regulae*) and content of Christian belief and to become philosophically acute in the process. Included in this process was the identification of a canon, or "rule," of scripture which eventually limited the number of approved New Testament books to twenty-seven—not without struggle and not without confusion.[5]

Heretical books were more easily excluded from the emerging canon because the theologies they embodied originated in groups or sects (thus, *haireses*: a school of thought) and were used chiefly against the "orthodox" as propaganda for the sect. But there was a sizeable body of literature which—unlike the Nag Hammadi papyri—managed to survive on the outskirts of orthodoxy. Neither heretical nor orthodox, these books are best described as a popularization of literary and doctrinal themes gleaned from the books of assured reputation. This type of literature exists for both the Old and the New Testaments, and is usually referred to as *apocrypha*. The term itself is now so widely misused and misunderstood that it will help to say a few words here about the sort of literature that is usually designated "apocryphal."

Although the term "apocryphal" is commonly understood to mean something that is untrue or highly questionable, it originally seems to have been used to designate a book too sacred to be placed in the hands of the ordinary believer.[6] The term originates as one of respect. It is St. Jerome (342–420) (to whom we owe one of the most important compilations and translations of the Bible, the Latin Vulgate) who is responsible for the way we think about apocryphal books today. For it was Jerome who applied the term to all books he regarded as being of "uncertain" authorship, and thus to be distinguished from books whose authorship was, so he thought, certainly apostolic.

And herein lies the problem. Christian writers before Jerome had made "apostolicity" the main criterion for the status of Christian books. Simply stated, this meant that if a book could be shown to come from the hands of a follower of Jesus, its prestige and authority were guaranteed. Irenaeus stresses in his *Against the Heresies* (ca. 180) a tradition that goes back at least to the time of the presbyter Papias (ca. 95); namely, that the four gospels—the number that is not seriously challenged beyond the late second century—should be believed because their authors were selected to tell the good news by Christ himself while he was still on earth, and that after his ascension, he imbued them and their work with the Holy Spirit as a guarantee of their truth. How different it is with heretics, Irenaeus exclaims: They rely partly on unwritten and secret tradition; they are never willing to acknowledge the source of their opinions, saying instead it comes to them by private revelation.[7] The gnostics in particular worried Irenaeus, because they seemed to reject the historical tradition implied in the doctrine of apostolic authorship and to attribute their sacred writings to distant and arcane "powers" to which no historical test could be applied. The Nag Hammadi discovery[8]—despite some claims to the contrary—have proved the accuracy of Irenaeus's representations. The gnostics were fond of citing the *Gospel of Truth* and the *Logia Iesou* (*Words of Jesus*) to weigh against the "human" compositions of the orthodox teachers. While it is true that there are "attributed" books among the gnostic scriptures (the most famous being the *Gospel of Thomas*, assigned in a prescript to Thomas, the Twin of John 20) the content even of the gnostic books attributed to historical authors, as the name of the movement connotes, is historically fuzzy and theo-sophically complex,[9] and their difference from the gospels that have come down to us in the New Testament canon is plain to see. The quarrel between Irenaeus and his successor bishops and the gnostics was, with respect to the Bible anyway, a quarrel over the sources of authority: namely, whether that authority was to be understood historically, as through the orthodox doctrine of apostolic author-ship, or supernaturally, as in the gnostic doctrine of "secret" reve-lation by the savior-revealer.

In arguing their case, the bishops were forced into certain com-promises. Again to take the case of the second-century bishop Ire-naeus: He is happy to employ the tradition, against the heretics, that John, the beloved disciple, wrote the Fourth Gospel as well as all other books, including the Apocalypse, that go under his name. And he is happy with the tradition that Matthew was the tax collector whose signature appears in the story of his call (Matt. 9.9ff.), even though the other synoptic writers (Luke 5.27f., Mark 2.13–17) name him Levi son of Alphaeus. In the case of authors whose names were not included in the lists of those called by Jesus, but whom tradi-tion names as writers of gospels, the task of establishing apostolic-ity became more problematical.

But Irenaeus was not working in the dark on this problem. He drew on an already old tradition that Mark had been the apostle Peter's traveling companion, and that Luke had been none other than the Luke mentioned by Paul (Col. 4.14) as his companion and a "dear doctor" (cf. 2 Tim. 4, 11; Philemon 23). In effect, the two nonapostles were made "apostolic" secretaries or apostolic men (*apostolici*) whose authority came directly from that of the great apostles and actually set in motion the apostolic teaching tradi-tion—of which the bishops themselves were thought to be heirs. The heretics (among their many other disadvantages) stood completely outside this tradition with their "ravings and idle speculation."[10]

In elevating apostolic authority in this way, in making authorship by an apostle the chief mark of correctness of content, the orthodox teachers undoubtedly meant to put a stop to spurious works
such as those created by the heretics. For better or worse, their pro-
nouncements and sallies against the heretics were effective, as the
growth of imperial Christianity, the gradual elimination of heretical
"cells," and even the burial (doubtless for safekeeping) of the texts
from Nag Hammadi go to show. The doctrine of *received tradition*
(*paradosis*) rooted in an institution and a historical process made
better sense in a succession-minded and authority-ridden world,
such as that of the late Roman empire, than the obscure theosophical cant of the gnostic teachers. The gnostic gospels, however, did
not fail to win acceptance simply because the bishops of the orthodox churches untiringly blasted them with important rhetoric. They
failed because at least some of the church fathers' broadsides were
right on target.

But the early Christian church, from at least the beginning of the
second century, was not all bishops, and even among the bishops
there were neologists and literary men. If the canon was on the
threshold of being closed by Irenaeus's day (ca. 180 C.E.), the faithful of the emergent Christian world were not aware of it. For one
thing, since most could not read, their "reading" of unapproved
books would have been an empty concern for the bishops. Much of
what was believed by grassroots Christians in the second century
came from Christian folklore and legend, the greater part of it delivered orally, and not from a canon.[11] In dealing with the issue of
the canon, therefore, the bishop-teachers of the second and third
centuries had one eye on consensus (which meant on each other)
and another on rival teachers, heretics, and pagans. The greatest
spur to forming a canon other than the rivalry itself was the need to
assert clearly to the pagan world—a world of religio-philosophical
sophistication where precedent, antiquity, and historical ground-

edness mattered considerably—what body of literature should be considered definitely Christian. The answer was fairly simple: that literature which was commissioned by Christ, dictated through the spirit, written by apostolic men, and explained by their successors. Such logic did not, of course, quell the pagan criticism of the new faith, nor stem the proliferation of dissident opinion (heresy), but the logic itself was perfectly sound.

It may be wondered whether the bishops possessed a third eye for the faithful. The answer is hard to come by. It is certain that the nonheretical apocryphal books were written by educated, if not talented, Christians, and, since one of the requirements for a bishop (1 Tim. 3.2) is that he be "an apt teacher," some educated Christians were bishops. It follows, therefore, that some of the apocryphal New Testament books may have been written by bishops. But why were they written, given the fact that the church was in a hurry to define itself through more sober reflection and teaching, against the heretics and for the pagans?

M. R. James, in his 1924 anthology of apocryphal texts, submitted that they were written in order "to reinforce the existing stock of Christian beliefs: either by revealing new doctrines . . . or by interpreting old ones."[12] They were written, first of all, as a kind of supplementary history—but history of a special sort, which served the devotional needs of a Christian community already in possession of canonical texts and traditions. The more patently heretical books— the gnostic *Gospel of Thomas,* for example—served no such clientele. Their purchase was on the life of a cult, a community of the enlightened, with theologically tortuous doctrines of fall and redemption. But the literature of the Christian canon seemed to speak of the here and now, of "the things which have happened among us," and of which an "orderly account" could be made (Luke 1.1, 3). True, one among the four—John's gospel—seemed more de-

23

tached, more speculative, than the others. But in the version in which it was most widely known, it, too, made a boast about its witness, its historical grounding, even the comprehensiveness, of its report (John 20.30; 21.20ff.), and its account of the passion of Jesus on the cross is a positive taunt to the gnostic doctrine of a selfish, spiritually agonized, but physically unperturbed savior-revealer. The gnostic literature could be indefinitely supplemented because gnostic revelation had not been located in any specific sense in the time when Quirinius was governor of Syria and Herod was tetrarch of Judaea. The historical markers, like the biographical demarcations of birth and death, or the genealogies contrived by Matthew and Luke to end the slander about Jesus' parentage,[13] were significantly lacking in the gnostic gospels.

But not *all* supplements to the canonical literature lacked historical or biographical interest. The apocryphal literature was partly a response to a craving for greater biographical detail—for more of the "Jesus story" than the canonical sources, in their concrete realization after the second century, were able to provide. As supplementary sources, grounded in the devotional life of churches rather than in heretical cells, they were judged by a different set of criteria than those applied to canonical writings. The apocryphal books were seen to be connected loosely to apostolic traditions and to be linked to central doctrines of the Christian faith. Even though their claim to apostolic legitimacy was tenuous, they had defenders as well as critics.[14] With respect to attribution, the books resemble Jewish *midrashim* and the Old Testament apocrypha. To secure authority or credibility, they are written under the honorary name of an apostle or some other prominent figure. Put flatly, they are forged, but then so are many of the canonical New Testament books—and for just the same reason. Thus we possess "gospels" attributed to James, Peter, Bartholomew, Mary, and Nicodemus; Acts of Peter,

Paul, John, Andrew and Thomas, and Pontius Pilate; apocalypses of Peter, Paul, and Thomas. The list is as impressive as the ascriptions are unconvincing. Though individual bishops cite them and credit the authorship traditions selectively, they are clearly regarded as subordinate in authority to canonical texts. With respect to content, the apocryphal books were "marginally" orthodox, even within an era of doctrinal crenulation. I do not mean by this that they express orthodox beliefs or comport at every turn with the content of canonical writings. Clearly this is not the case. Rather, their at-variance is more often than not a matter of inadvertence, exaggeration, or plain sloppiness rather than a case of willfully revising or challenging orthodox belief in the way gnostic gospels did. At worst, they are theatrically expansive—a case of what Aristotle might have called "failed magnitude." But at their best, the apocryphal books are simple, entertaining, and revealing. They were recognized as such until the Reformation, as their popularity as a source of dramatic themes in the Middle Ages serves to illustrate.

The apocryphal books' theatricality is a feature of the second purpose for which they were written: to be works of religious devotion. It is arguable that many of them started as sermons. We know certainly of their currency among homilists of the fourth century such as Cyril of Jerusalem, Demetrius of Antioch, the ardent heresy-fighter Epiphanius, and Cyril of Alexandria. Whether they "composed" gospels to suit their sermons or sermons that drew on extracanonical gospels we cannot now know. But it is certain that preachers from the second to the fourth century knew the value of folklore, legend, and tall tale in spicing a sermon, and made free use of what they heard or read.

It is also pretty certain that the main test a homilist would have applied to the apocrypha was that of *plausibility.* A book attributed to a significant New Testament personage which did not expressly contradict the content of the gospels or the teaching of the church was not regarded as heretical but *disputandum* (unproved), more with respect to authorship than substance. For example, there is nothing especially shocking about the account of Christ's descent into hell in the third-century *Gospel of Nicodemus*. Almost all Christians of the period believed that Christ "harrowed" (descended into and evacuated) hell in the time between his crucifixion and resurrection. The fathers of the church uniformly believed in the episode, differing only as to the reasons for the descent and who was harrowed. The so-called Apostles' Creed included the doctrine, while Nicaea eliminated it from the creed written there and the very late New Testament writing known as 1 Peter (3.19) refers to Christ preaching to the spirits imprisoned [in the underworld]. But despite the vague allusion in 1 Peter, the doctrine derives largely from its apocryphal expression in the *Gospel of Nicodemus*, from which a little can be quoted:

> *Satan* then said to *Hell*, "Get ready to accept the man I am bringing down to you."
> And *Hell* answered *Satan*, "The voice I heard can only have come from the son of the most high Father. Why, all the regions of hell are shaken at it. I am worried that my bonds will split open, and so I beg of you, Satan, prince of evil, by all that's in you—and in me—don't bring this man to me, lest we become captives ourselves."[15]

The comic confusion of soon-to-be confounded powers of death is evident. The content of the gospel is elaborate, but not unorthodox. It is the embodiment in "gospel" of the details one would normally expect of a sermon or a play.[16] Its ascription to Nicodemus (John 3.1ff.), the Pharisee who came to Jesus by night, was not especially convincing, however; and so it, along with the other so-called Acts of Pilate, was finally shoved aside.[17] Most of the apocryphal literature is of a similar kind, as references in the church fathers, especially Jerome, the Gelasian Decree of the fifth century, and the Stichometry of Nicephorus make clear: they are pointedly referred to as "disputed" books (in the Stichometry, so is the now canonical Revelation of John), and of a stature close to that of the so-called *Epistle of Barnabas* and the *Shepherd of Hermas*, both of which were accorded great respect prior to the fourth century. Their very ambiguity in these lists is one explanation of their survival. But, for the most part, their survival must be explained by their popular appeal.

Like stained glass and baroque frill, the apocryphal books are ornamental in nature. For their creators, the approved stock of Christian gospels only imperfectly embodied or supported beliefs and practices that had become central to the devotional life of the church. The author of the *Book of James,* for example, is dissatisfied with the evangelist's cryptic assertion of Mary's virginity by Matthew; he is responding to a need—his own or his congregation's—for a fuller account of the tantalizingly vague clause, "She found she was with child by the holy spirit." The author of the infancy *Gospel of Thomas*—not to be confused with the gnostic *Gospel of Thomas*—is likewise eager for a full account of Jesus' infancy and lost years, before he "was about thirty years old" (Luke 3.23).

The reasons for wanting fuller accounts are obvious even at our own historical distance from the events recorded in the gospels. Documents crafted in one historical context behave differently in another. It would be fair to say that Matthew regards the virgin birth as worth mentioning because he sees it as the fulfillment of a particular messianic prophecy.[18] Luke, though he does not link the birth to a prophetic text, sees the status of Mary as being enhanced by God's selection of her as the Christ-bearer (cf. Luke 1.46–55). In this process, Mary becomes an object of devotion in her own right and her Magnificat, or song of acceptance (a poetic text adapted for

Christian use from 1 Samuel 2.1–10), a programmatic text in Marian cult devotion. The author of the *Book of James* and the authors of the several Assumptions of the Virgin build on the gospel tradition to accommodate the devotional life of their day and time.

The apocryphal writers do not seem to have wished to subtract from the integrity or authority of the gospels they expanded, or to replace them (as the gnostics did) with "new revelation," since they obviously regarded the received books as authoritative in the first place. The apocryphal supplements can be considered, at this third level, embellishments of canonical material tailored to suit the devotional life of their communities. Whether there were more sinister or crass aims involved in their composition is difficult to determine. The author of Luke's gospel was, apparently, paid by Theophilus for the story he wrote in two installments (Acts 1.1)—or, rather, borrowed from other sources (Luke 1.2f.). Hence, there is no reason to suppose that some apocryphal texts were not composed for curious pagan patrons who could afford to pay for sequels to the Jesus story of the gospels.[19] Inevitably these stories bear the stamp of the communities or *patrones* for which they were composed, in Rome, Greece and the eastern Empire, Egypt, and Armenia. The "regionalism" of the apocryphal traditions—differing styles for differing literary and devotional tastes—sets them apart from the synoptic and Johannine sources, which, despite their linguistic and theological disparities, tend to look very much alike to the untrained eye. The sameness of the canonical texts (John's gospel being a significant exception) gained them the acceptance of a wide audience throughout the empire within a generation or two after their composition. Large segments of the apocryphal tradition, on the other hand, remained stubbornly local.

What is stated matter-of-factly and briefly in the canonical gospels—that Mary was a virgin, that Jesus was obedient to them in Nazareth, or that Jesus on one occasion confounded the wisdom of the wise—become literary opportunities for the authors of the apocrypha. Meditation and homilizing on such "facts" was a normal part of church life in the second and third centuries, periods of erratic persecution for many Christians. Tales of the miraculous, especially stories of the impudent boy-savior who could wither his enemies, physical or intellectual, with only a glance or a word, would have been especially appealing in such a context. The appetite for such stories would have been an encouragement to storytellers with a political agenda in view. At this level, the hermetic Christ child of the secret gospels is a warning to the enemies of the church, Jewish and pagan, that God deals harshly with his enemies.

The apocryphal New Testament literature is heavy with the miraculous. Its touchstone is the canonical literature, but any reader of, say, the infancy stories of *Thomas* will notice the increased emphasis on raw, sometimes cynical displays of the power of God through a precocious infant savior. If such stories were known to the evangelists at all, as some may have been to Luke (cf. 2.44ff., and *perhaps* Mark 11.12–14) or an editor of his gospel, they were excluded for the very cynicism which the author of *Thomas* finds compelling.

Still on the eve of the Reformation, cycles of plays such as those at Coventry, York, and Townley in England, exploited the apocryphal stories for their dramatic and theatrical potential. One of these is the fifteenth-century *Ludus Coventriae*, a "mystery" (liturgical) cycle performed annually at the feast of Corpus Christi. Its elements include the story of the conception of Mary, the life of Mary in the Temple, her betrothal to Joseph, the "parliament" in heaven prior to the Annunciation, Joseph's jealousy and anger at finding his betrothed with child, the trial of Joseph and Mary—and much else besides.[20]

If these "elements" sound foreign to a context whose other parts are taken from canonical books, that is because the author of the plays followed the medieval pattern of borrowing freely from the apocryphal sources. A fourteenth-century poem known as the *Cursor Mundi*, written in the Northumbrian dialect, makes use of traditions that can be traced all the way back to Arabic infancy stories from the fifth century and perhaps to earlier Syriac sources. This, for example, is its view of the Flight into Egypt:

> Forth she rode, the maiden mild,
> In her arm she laid her child,
> Till they came by a cave deep
> Where they thought to rest and sleep.
> The holy pair prepared to light
>
> > When they saw an awful sight.
> > As they looked askance, beside:
> > Out of the cave they saw glide
> > Many dragons suddenly.
> > The parents quivered fearfully
> > Till Jesus saw they frightened be;
> > He went down from his mother's knee
> > And stood afront the beasts so grim
> > And the beasties worshiped him.[21]

In the Arabic original, the holy family is shown fleeing the wrath of Herod (also a favorite dramatic topic); they pause to rest when "suddenly many dragons come out of a cave" and those thereabout cry in terror. Jesus stands down from his mother's lap before the dragons and they worship him, in fulfillment of Psalm 148.7, misquoted by the author to read "Praise the Lord, you dragons from the earth."[22] But, of course, the medieval writer of mystery plays did not know the Arabic original. He knew rather the devotional tradition of the Church into which the story had long since passed.

The Reformation, with its battle cry of "Scripture alone!" and insistence on maintaining the boundaries between scripture and church tradition, marks the end of such emoluments.[23] But for the faithful of the Middle Ages, lettered and unlearned alike, the stock of Christian legend was much greater than we today know it to be. Their mosaic of the history of salvation was not confined to the books that the bishops of the fourth century or reformers in the sixteenth were in a hurry to catalogue and limit. Even Muhammad knew (and credited) many of the infancy stories from the apocryphal tradition, and the Quran makes use of a number of them.[24]

The key to understanding the apocryphal books is to understand their role in the life of ordinary believers. As post-Reformation, and, in many instances, post-Christian, women and men, we are accustomed to using the canonical New Testament literature as the balance against which to weigh all material that falls outside the limits history has imposed. Even so adept a student of the apocrypha as M. R. James could aver that the apocryphal materials "fail in their purpose." That may indeed be true for us, but it is probably not true of *it*—of the literature considered purely in terms of the influence it exerted, in its own time, on popular devotion and Christian belief. James was forced to acknowledge that while their authors do not exhibit the temperance of the evangelists or Paul, "they record the imaginations, hopes and fears of [those] who wrote them; they show what was acceptable to the unlearned Christians of the first ages, what they admired, what ideals of conduct they cherished for this life, and what they thought they would find in the next."[25]

Even so, one of the difficulties we encounter in approaching the apocryphal books for the first time, quite apart from the historical question of canonicity, is that ideals of conduct and "what we admire" have changed considerably since the books were written. Churchgoers in many traditions have become accustomed to a demythologized Christianity, in which the role of the supernatural, the miraculous, and the strange have been shoved to the margins of

31

Christian preaching and replaced by an emphasis on the social and
ethical aspects of the gospels. In the new dispensation, the rele-
vance of the gospels is seen to have less to do with who Jesus was—
a man whose power and authority derived from God, his father—
than with the agendas to which elements of his teaching can be
applied. In this context, the amorality and blunt divinity of the
apocryphal Jesus is a discomfort, since it reminds us of the prickly
and disinterested parabolist of Mark 4, who announces to his disciples that his teaching is meant to confuse anyone who is not his
follower, or the fatigued traveler who curses a fig tree for failing to
bear fruit out of season (Mark 11.12–14). It is perhaps too facile a
solution to the problem of the apocryphal gospels to say that they are
morally inferior (thus James) to canonical texts, since the beliefs
they express also represent the standard beliefs of a Christian community who revered the "approved" books. That community belonged to a world in which calming angry seas, curing diseased
souls, and raising the dead to life were more relevant components
of the religious life than the amelioration of social injustice. It re-
spected the teaching of the savior, but demanded the miraculous of
him as well. It was religiously fixated on the mysteries of incarnation and divinity and virgin birth: in a phrase, it worshiped Christ
as God.[26] It revered his mother almost as greatly as it did him—so
much so that her virginity came to be seen not only as a comment
on *his* divine stature but as a hallowing of her humanity. She becomes, through the pious logic of the incarnation, Mary conceived
without sin,[27] the God-bearer, the heavenly woman who is spared
death and decay by the intervention of her son.[28]

The modern world does not admire virginity for its own sake.
The ancient world, including the ancient Christian world, did. The
author of the *Book of James* writes in support of belief in the perpetual virginity of Mary—a belief widespread already by the second
century and generalized from the seventh century with a feast in

32

honor of her miraculous conception. Neither Matthew nor Luke says a word about the parentage of Mary, but her role as the "new Eve" is already asserted by Christian fathers in the second century and her cult grows rapidly thereafter. Medieval theologians like Anselm and Abelard—themselves no friends of literary frippery—speculate on the doctrinal gravity of Mary's sinlessness, though it is nowhere stated in canonical books. In the *Book of James* the cult is given, so to speak, its own "pre-gospel" (hence, *Protevangelium*) of the Blessed Virgin which emphasizes her personal purity and favor in God's eyes as a necessary condition of the privilege she is granted, that of being the mother of the son of God. In the process, the writer extols her virtue and the virtue of chastity as models of Christian living. She is not only a remarkable child who walks at six months and learns to embroider soon after, but her voice is the envy of the doves who perch on her window ledge. Thereafter, she is the confused teenager who does not understand why God would single her out (cf. Luke 1.34), the obedient servant (handmaid) of the Lord, a refugee from Joseph's house as she contemplates his re-action to her pregnancy, and finally the mother who glories in her child and the care of her family. While she sometimes benefits and sometimes suffers (like Maia of Cyllene, the virgin mother of Hermes) from demonstrations of the infant Jesus' powers, the task of discipline, insofar as it is emphasized at all, is left to Joseph.

In the Joseph tradition, also included here, the pattern is the same. The sources from the Eastern church, largely from Egypt where the cult of *Mar*-Iusef (Saint Joseph) enjoyed early popularity, emphasize that Joseph was a righteous man who had been married before, to a woman named Salome, a kinswoman of Mary, and had by his first wife four sons (the names vary: often Judas, Joses, Simon, and James) and two daughters (Lysia, or Aszia, and Lydia). James is said to have been "very young" when Joseph's wife died. In keeping with the general Near Eastern pattern of such tales, the special relationship—though never asserted to be biological—between James and Jesus is thought to confer special status on James as a witness and reporter.[29]

The Joseph tradition is clearly subordinate to the Marian: once the perpetual virginity of Mary had become an object of devotion, it became a matter of some concern to insist on the sanctity of Joseph and the chasteness of the marital arrangement organized by the priests. It became necessary as well to explain miscellaneous gospel references to the "brothers and sisters" of Jesus. Mark 3.21 records that Jesus' "relations" tried to seize him "because he was beside himself." John 7.3–5 reports that the brothers of Jesus "had no faith in him" and wanted him to seek his fortune in Jerusalem, while the (apocryphal) Gospel of the Nazarenes presents Mary and the brothers of Jesus urging him to submit to the baptism of John. Above all, there is the passage in Mark 6.3, in which Jesus' countrymen refer to him as "the carpenter, the son of Mary, the brother of James and Joses and Judas and Simon," and mention "his sisters here with us." Without belaboring the obvious difficulty of squaring these references as they stand in the gospels with belief in the perpetual virginity of Mary, the solution to the doctrinal puzzle they create could be sought in the nature of the conjugal tie between Mary and Joseph and specifically in Joseph's history prior to the betrothal, a history about which the gospels are silent.

In the logic of devotion, which is the logic of the Joseph tradition, Mary's virginity entails Joseph's righteousness. In imagining this relationship, there was some canonical support: He is a just man (*dikaios*) unwilling to make a public example of her (Matt. 1.19f.). In the apocryphal tradition, he becomes a widower with six children, some still living at home. His trade, perhaps mistakenly derived from a conflation of Luke 4.22 and Matt. 13.55, is that of a carpenter, and in a romantic vision it is this trade that he teaches

34

the young Jesus in his shop in Nazareth. Joseph's unwillingness to expose Mary as an adultress ( the Talmudic tradition, known also to Matthew: 1.18f.) does not diminish his confusion in finding her pregnant, and this, too—the anguish of Joseph—becomes a source for romantic elaboration in the apocryphal books.

Finally there is the question of upbringing. The Gospel of Luke suggests that Jesus was "subject" to the authority of Mary and Joseph in Nazareth (Luke 2.51), but the Greek term (*hypotassomenos*) implies willing subjection. Clearly this was no ordinary boy, and his obedience to his parents was early seen as a case of divine condescension. The boy Jesus is therefore represented as being tolerant of the authority of Joseph on the human level, while causing his father considerable trouble with his periodic flashes of divine distemper. In essence, Joseph is the ideal guardian-protector and Jesus (with exceptions) the model of filial obedience. Joseph is seen as a man too old to be interested in Mary's natural beauty, and promises the priests her safety and well-being in his care. In the Egyptian tradition, he is forty when he *first* marries and is married to his first wife for forty-nine years. After a year alone following his wife's death, Joseph was with Mary for two years before the nativity of Jesus, making him ninety-two or so at the time.

It will be clear from what has already been said that the apocryphal infancy gospels serve at a fourth level to reinforce certain beliefs that are only briefly or implicitly identified in the canonical gospels, or to support doctrines—like that of the perpetual virginity of Mary—which might be seen as insupportable in terms of other canonical evidence (cf. Matt. 1.18 and Matt. 13.55–56). A theological interest rather than a purely narrative impulse or hankering for biography is the spur to their formation. Yet the narrative impulse is much more prominent in the apocryphal infancy stories than in the infancy portions of Matthew and Luke. In the latter, the two evangelists offer their different accounts in order to maintain the theological proposition that God revealed himself in Christ "so directly that a unity of will and being must be assumed." The canonical writers pointed to Jesus' birth to a virgin, God's intrusion into the natural order, to explain this unity without quite managing, in the classical style, a virgin birth story (like that told of the emperor Augustus by Asclepias of Mendes). Jesus' Davidic genealogy, his birth in Bethlehem, the adoptive paternity of Joseph, the status of canonical references to brothers and sisters, and the fulfillment of Old Testament prophecies are, in various ways, attached to this proposition, so that from a purely theological point of view it is impossible not to think of the birth of Jesus as the critical story of God's revelation of his will and purpose.

Once this proposition is established—that the birth of Jesus is the concrete *moment* of the incarnation—the way is paved for the more purely narrative interest which the apocryphal writers show. The curiosity of the believer combines with the natural desire of the storyteller to satisfy the curious, or the duty of the preacher to teach doctrine to the faithful. For the early Christian church, the *Book of James* "taught" the virgin birth much more vividly and convincingly than did the gospels of Matthew and Luke.

Legends, however, are not without an interest in the everyday and commonplace affairs of life, and in the infancy legends the incidence of the commonplace increases: Zechariah, the husband of Mary's cousin Elizabeth and Joseph's literary "twin," is a laughingstock because he cannot father sons; Elizabeth goes through a period of depression because her husband seems to have deserted her; Mary's parents, Joachim and Anna, despite their promises to God, cannot bear the thought of parting with the two-year-old prodigy God has given them; Joseph openly feels betrayed that Mary has become pregnant by another man in his absence; and the young Jesus grieves publicly by his pseudo-father's bedside at

Joseph's death. These "human" touches are not prominent in the canonical sources, and their increase in the apocrypha can be explained only by looking to the audience for whom the accounts were composed. On the whole, they were the average Christians of the third and fourth centuries, whose everyday concerns and values found an echo in the tribulations of the family of Jesus.

Inevitably, the same audience was much devoted to the miraculous. Zechariah is struck dumb by an angel for doubting God; Elizabeth, Mary, and Joseph are the recipients of angelic visitations; God intervenes to end Elizabeth's infertility presumably through natural means, but in the conception of Jesus preserves Mary's virginity; Joseph's anointed role as husband is confirmed by the apparition of a dove that emerges from his staff; Mary walks at six months; and the newborn Christ, like the newborn Hermes, is able to perform cures only minutes after his birth.

Most people who have some familiarity with the apocryphal tradition especially represented by the infancy *Gospel of Thomas* and Arabic sources are eager to insist on the divine powers of the Christ child. The swaddling clothes of Jesus prove to be fireproof; Egyptian idols fall from their place in a temple; demon-serpents flee in the child's presence; dragons adore him; at Matatieh the child's sweat causes a spring to burst forth; and in Misr (Cairo), where the family bides for three years, he impresses Pharoah with "many miracles not recorded in the Gospel of the Infancy."

Once the family is settled in Nazareth (or Bethlehem), the legends of Jesus' divine powers become the focus of the stories. Doubtless because of the canonical view that Jesus was later on rejected in his home town (Mark 6.4 pars.), the apocryphal gospels commonly insist (in direct contrast to their sources) that the family was persecuted on account of Jesus' random displays of thaumaturgy and magic. Joseph arranges a succession of teachers for the child, most of whom come to a bad end when they discover that Jesus is wise far beyond his years and human capacity. The source for the tales seems to be Luke 2.46f., the discovery of Jesus teaching the "doctors" in the Temple. But it is just possible that Luke—or one of his editors—was himself drawing on a very early infancy tradition (if not Christian, then certainly pagan) in composing his account.

Beyond the tradition of Jesus' education in letters, the Nazareth years see his development as a healer and worker of signs. The *Book of James* contains the most famous of the infancy stories (also known to Muhammad): the infant's forming living sparrows out of clay, an ingenious way of underscoring his status as the creative Word of God present in the making of the world (John 1.1–2). Jesus' occasional smiting of playmates and others who have offended him is meant to illustrate his role as judge. It is normally offset by healings and restorations of those who ask for his forgiveness and mercy, illustrating still another aspect of the divine persona. The Greek god Hermes is similarly required to restore Apollo's cows in order to pacify his father, Zeus.

Undoubtedly, however, the writers go beyond the mere amplification of theological attributes: In one Arabic account, two mothers come to Jesus with ailing children. One child (named Cleopas) is healed, the other dies, whereupon the mother of the dead child throws Cleopas into an oven and then into a well. Cleopas survives it all unharmed, but the wicked mother of the dead child herself falls into the well and is killed. With time comes elaboration. The *Gospel of Thomas* elaborates its canonical sources, and infancy gospels built upon *Thomas* show a marked increase of legendary material. In Syriac lives of the virgin and in the Arabic infancy tradition, Jesus is represented as a figure of Olympian stature—again, like the young Hermes, a trickster who delights in showing off his supernatural skills. Thus, his swaddling clothes can be used to ward off dragons; a boy possessed by the devil (coincidentally named Judas) who strikes Jesus and is exorcised, beholds the devil

fleeing in the form of a dog; the story of the making of the clay sparrows becomes one about creating a menagerie of animals, who then
come to life and go their way. The increase in legendary material
shows that the motives of the composers of these gospels were
mixed. On the one hand, they must have believed that what they
were doing supported the doctrine that Jesus, as the son of God, was
capable of extraordinary feats. By the same token, much of what we
find in gospels written in the fourth, fifth, and sixth centuries would
seem to suggest an interest in the "entertainment value" of the
story form, and it is that value, finally, which determines the survival of the apocryphal tradition in the Middle Ages.

This survival is nothing short of marvelous in its own right, con-
sidering the amount of official energy spent trying to bring the cir-
culation of apocryphal gospels under control. In the West, Jerome
pressed for condemnation of the texts under three successive popes:
Damasus, Innocent I, and Gelasius. The much-disputed "Gelasian
Decree" of the fifth (?) century, titled *De libris recipiendis et non recipiendis (Of the books to be received and not to be received)* can probably be traced in part to Pope Damasus himself (366–84); it certainly
mentions the "Book about the Childhood of the Redeemer," and the
"Book about the Birth of the Redeemer and about Mary or the Midwife," designations which would correspond to the *Book of James*
and to the infancy *Gospel of Thomas*. Many other apocryphal books
—gospels, acts, collections, and martyrologies—are included in the
decree. But in practical terms, the decree did little to remove the
apocryphal traditions from the popular consciousness or even from
the preaching life of the church. The twelfth-century monk St. Aelred
of Rievaulx has this to say in one of his spiritual reflections:

> Doubt not that when he had fled into Egypt, the Lord was cap-
> tured by robbers and saved by the kindness of the son of one of
> them. It is said that the one who saved him was no other than the

son of the chief of the robbers, and it happened this way: the robber's son beheld the infant at its mother's breast, and such radiance appeared in his face that he could not doubt that the infant
was more than mortal, and so he held him and said, "Greatly
blessed child, if ever there should come a time when you can return the mercy I now show you, do not forget me." And it is said
that this robber's son is none other than the thief who was crucified on Christ's right hand.[30]

The further success of the tradition is amply illustrated by the
popularity of apocryphal motifs in medieval drama and poetry, as
well as in homily and hymn. In the sixteenth century, Pope Pius V
attempted to scrap the Feast of St. Joachim, the father of Mary according to the apocryphal tradition, as well as the Feast of the Presentation of Mary in the Temple, known only from the apocryphal
*Book of James.* Popular devotion to the feasts was such, however,
that they were reestablished, the latter by Sixtus V in 1585. In the
Eastern Church, the Presentation is one of the Twelve Great Feasts
of the church year. Luther, who later became a critic of the apocryphal books as "Latin fictions," himself had become a monk "at the
summons of St. Anne, mother of Mary."

Oscar Cullmann has said that in antiquity, the Middle Ages, and
the Renaissance, the apocryphal infancy narratives "exercised more
influence on literature and art than the Bible itself." One has only
to think of the Latin hymns of the jurist Prudentius (348–410) or the
praise-songs of the medieval nun Hroswitha (Hrosvit) of Saxony
(10th cent.), both of whom employ the legends of the so-called
Gospel of Pseudo-Matthew along with canonical materials without
distinction. Early and medieval Christian art borrowed heavily from
the infancy gospels, the miracles performed by Jesus just after his
birth, the luminosity of the cave, and the scene of Mary spinning for
the Temple curtain being favorite motifs. In the ninth century,

*Introduction*

Leo III ordered the Church of St. Paul in Rome to be decorated with the whole story of Joachim and Anna. Hence, the apocryphal writings' popularity and influence can be assumed throughout the greater period of the church's history.

This brief introduction brings us to the present work. It began with my desire to produce critical editions of the Coptic and Arabic apocryphal gospels. That task continues. But in the process of doing the essential work of reading and translation, it occurred to me that a different sort of project would be worthwhile, one which would make selections of these influential books available to modern readers who may not be familiar with the Christian apocryphal literature. Once the decision was made, I encountered a difficulty: how should the materials be put together? As most theologians and scholars in the field of early Church history know, the infancy tradition is diffuse and long-lived, continuing as an "active" compositional genre as late as the tenth century when Hroswitha of Gandersheim in Saxony wrote poetic paraphrases of a *Liber de infantia,* otherwise known as the Gospel of the Pseudo-Matthew. How much of the infancy tradition should be presented? It is too much to expect the interested or even the curious reader to sort out the complex history of the genre, but it will make my arrangement clearer and more defensible if I can say just the following.

First, it is probably impossible to fix a dividing line between the canonical accounts and the earliest of the apocryphal infancy stories. Our earliest references to the latter in the writings of Justin Martyr suggest that a thriving genre existed already in the second century. Second, the genre seems to have flourished both in the Eastern and in the Western Church. The *Book of James* is mentioned by Origen (185–254), who cites the report that the "brothers of the Lord" were sons of Joseph by a former marriage, and Clement of Alexandria (150–215) mentions the tradition that a midwife was present at the nativity. These folkloristic elements can perhaps be traced back to the end of the first century and are given a permanent lease on life in the books attributed to James, the son of Joseph, and Thomas, the disciple of the Lord. In the seven centuries between Clement and Hroswitha, the genre flourishes throughout the church, as reflected in the variety of languages in which infancy gospels, whole or part, have come down to us: Greek, Syriac, Latin, Armenian, Coptic, and Arabic.

Translation often means expansion and elaboration. As the infancy gospels are themselves elaborations of canonical material, so each new writer and copyist tended to add fresh detail wherever he or she thought it would serve a purpose. This means that there is a great deal of repetition, or "doubling," of episodes, as well as episodes (especially in the Pseudo-Matthew) that cannot be traced to the earliest of the infancy narratives.

While this sort of complexity must be accounted for in scholarly translations and editions, it is the sort of thing that tends to make critical editions intimidating and/or tedious for the general reader. This book is, therefore, something of a compromise, but one offered with the nonspecialist in view. The title declares it to be a "harmony," that is, a continuous narrative built up from the various ancient sources, rather than a word-for-word translation of individual books. I have decided on this format for a number of reasons, chiefly to reduce the incidence of repetition and to give the work a coherence and unity that is completely missing from the anthologies of material now available.

But there is another reason for doing it this way. The work of harmonizing has a long history in the Christian church and has sometimes had interesting results. In the second century, an Assyrian presbyter named Tatian compiled an edition of the four gospels designed to provide a continuous narrative arranged so as to include all of the most important elements from the individual books. In Syriac churches, the *diatessaron* (one-from-four) arrangement was standard down to the fifth century, when the canonical order of four separate gospels was adopted. But from time to time, "harmonies" of the three synoptics and the Fourth Gospel have been attempted, often for apologetic reasons and other times for the sake of literary comprehension. In the present case, the harmony permits us to incorporate material from early and later sources and to offer a broad view of the seven-century spread of material with which we are dealing. What is lost in this procedure I feel is regained in having before us a rich tapestry of church tradition and a reasonably coherent chapter in the devotional life of Christianity. At the same time, the harmony avoids repetition and superfluous detail, and smoothes the disparities which occur in the variorum, or "variant," readings of particular sources.

In compiling this harmony I have referred to the best critical editions of important works in their original languages. Those interested in pursuing these sources will find the bibliographical note following the text helpful. Still, what is contained in these pages is neither a literal translation of these sources nor a paraphrase, but something more on the order of a retelling based, rather strictly, on the language, themes, and worldview of the originals. I have tried to impose some degree of order on unruly and episodic texts, beginning with the history of Joseph, moving then through the Mariological material of the *Book of James* and its dependent texts, and finally through the birth and infancy traditions of the *Gospel of Thomas* and the *Gospel of the Pseudo-Matthew,* and the traditions connected to these reports. In following this roughly biographical outline, I have sometimes resorted to the gospels of Matthew and Luke for guidance and wording, as the apocryphal writers themselves often did. The infancy stories are, after all, attempts in their own right to harmonize the variant synoptic accounts of the birth of Jesus as much as to supplement them. If I have been liberal in recomposing the tradition to provide a kind of literary wholeness, I hope that in so doing, I will have preserved and conveyed something of the spirit of these books. I have tried in the notes to keep the reader informed of the particular source being utilized as well as to provide essential information about the text. By doing this, I hope no one will feel unduly encumbered by these notes: in my view, the texts can be read and understood very well with much less documentation than I have provided here.

As to style, I can say that one of the most obvious features of the infancy stories generally is a certain literary naiveté. The authors may fancy themselves writers and poets, but on the whole they are not elegant stylists. Their work is marked by a kind of breathless impatience to get the story told, a circularity of narrative order, weakness of transition ("And soon after . . ."), and carelessness as to geographical and historical facts. These are the sorts of stories one would expect to hear in a playground or around a campfire; and yet even their stylistic innocence marks them off rather sharply from the contrived theosophical complexity of their gnostic cousins. The origin of the infancy tradition in popular devotion fully explains the literary shortcomings of *Thomas* and *James*, just as the cultic origins of the *Pistis Sophia* or *The Hypostasis of the Archons* explains the obsession of their authors with numbers, psychic eons, and secret names. The closest parallels to these stories must be sought in what nineteenth-century philologists would have called *Kleinliteratur*, i.e., fairy tale and folk story. At this rudimentary literary level, only a half step removed from the oral tradition and popular imagination, we can learn a great deal about the psychology of belief and the legend-making process generally. In view of this, I have done nothing to turn these little compositions into great literature. Where possible, I have tried to preserve the diction and syntax of the originals.

Those interested in dependable translations of the apocryphal sources now have an improved edition of M. R. James's *New Testa-*

*ment Apocrypha* by J. K. Elliott, which is described in the bibliographical note following the text.

I have also elected to provide two complementary kinds of material which, while not strictly a part of the infancy tradition, nonetheless spring directly from it. The first is what might be called the "Later History of the Holy Family." The substance of the *History of Joseph the Carpenter* is given here in its entirety, and divided into the story of the events in Joseph's life just prior to the birth of Jesus (chs. 1–11); then his birth and early childhood; and the story (chs. 12–32) of the sickness and death of Joseph, which was used in the Coptic church as a model of holy dying. The story is touching and occasionally beautiful. The Marian equivalent is the tradition of the "Assumption of the Virgin," a comprehensive description of which dates from the fourth century and survives in Greek, Latin, Syriac, and Coptic. It is now agreed that the belief does not date from the very earliest days of the church—St. Ambrose and St. Epiphanius know nothing about it. But once belief in the miraculous conception of Mary became current, propagated by the *Book of James* and through the various legends about St. John the Evangelist, belief in her physical elevation into heaven almost irresistibly followed. Like the Joseph-apocryphon, the belief in Mary's miraculous transit to heaven seems to reflect ancient Near Eastern and perhaps especially Coptic influence. In any event, the events of their deaths are intimately tied to their roles as foster-father and mother of the redeemer and in that sense complete the infancy cycle.

The second sort of material which I have felt it important to include is the Christ-Hymn. From the earliest days of the church, Christians sang songs, originally the Old Testament psalms and then hymns to Christ. One of the earliest of these is quoted by Paul in his letter to the Philippian Christians (Phil. 2.5–11), an incarnation hymn. Another very early example is the prologue of the Gospel of John, which is at least in part hymnic in structure. Both are given here in a translation which I think emphasizes their original purpose. They are followed by a "hymn" which is both fascinating and problematical, the so-called *Song of the Pearl*, originally written in Syriac and incorporated into the text of a lengthy apocryphal romance titled the *Acts of Thomas*. Its relation to the Philippian hymn and to the prologue remains to be closely identified, but its theme—the redeemer sent into a world of darkness which threatens to overcome him before his task is accomplished—is common to orthodox and to gnostic belief, even though its expression and theological bias differ radically. By the time of Jesus, it was a commonplace of Jewish speculation as well to think of God's "wisdom" in personified fashion as a woman sent into the world to call mankind to repentance.[31]

The apocryphal tradition is not a literature of ideas. It is not even first-class religious literature. The church's intellectuals, with a few notable exceptions, have not always been comfortable with the "devotional" church—the church of ordinary believers. (Would Thomas Aquinas have visited Lourdes if Lourdes had been around in his day?) The apocryphal tradition is the literature of ordinary belief, impassioned, unstructured, repetitious, naive. What one can see in these gospels are the undeveloped paths in Christian belief which, in choosing the canon it did, the Catholic church chose not to follow. In pursuing the apocryphal tradition, however, it is just as well to remember that these undeveloped paths follow by means of a crude literary logic from paths already laid out by the authors of the canonical books. In answering the question, What did Christians *believe* in the first centuries of the church's existence? reference must be made to both authorized and secret gospels.

# I

# A History of Joseph the Carpenter

And God looked down onto Bethlehem of Judah, the least promising of places, and he saw his servant Joseph. He was a righteous man, a carpenter by trade, with four sons: Judas, Josetos, James, and Simon, and two daughters, Aszia and Lydia. The carpenter's wife had died when James was still an infant.

As was his custom, Joseph, his sons and daughters, went up to Jerusalem for the Passover feast. On his arrival, a priest of the Temple came to him and said, "Joseph: there is a virgin living in the Temple, one whom God highly favors. You are a just man, and tomorrow, by lot, we will choose a husband for her." Joseph asked her age. "She is twelve," said the priest, but one far advanced in mind and heart—wise with the wisdom God alone can give."

Joseph prayed through the night. On the next day people gathered at the Temple to hear what the priests would say. The beauty of this girl was known to everyone and many men of Jerusalem had hoped to win her for a wife. "We have seen the will of God in the casting of lots for Mary, the virgin of the Temple. The lot has fallen to Joseph, a carpenter of Bethlehem and he will be her husband."

Joseph was an old man when the announcement was made, and straightaway he took Mary as his betrothed, with the blessing of the priests. A year had passed since his first wife's passing, and not wishing to take advantage of the girl, he did not insist that they sleep together as husband and wife. Mary loved James as her own child, the others being grown and able to care for themselves, but James she loved.

And so while still a girl she became known as Mary, "The Mother of James."

In the second year of their betrothal, Mary came to Joseph while he was busy in his workshop.

"Joseph," she said, "I am to have a child."

"But how?" he said. "I have not been a husband to you. You were a virgin when I took you into my house. For all I know, you are still innocent."

But Joseph was a fair man, and not wanting to disgrace her, he decided to go to the priests and to have the contract annulled.

That evening, once his mind was set on divorcing her, he thought he saw the angel Gabrhi-el, and the angel said to him "Do not be ashamed of her, Joseph: God came, and he entered her. The son she is bearing is none other than Joshua who shall save his people from sin."

"Is this Emmanu-el," thought Joseph, "the one Isaias foretold? The son of an innocent girl?"

"This is God among you," answered Gabrhi-el.

So Joseph rose from sleep, deeply troubled. But he took Mary home again, and decided to avoid the priests. He thought for a long time about the angel's story, and though she was his charge he refused to come near her until the time of the prophecy could be fulfilled.

And James was at Mary's feet, laughing, while Joseph pondered the angel's words.

Many years later, after Joseph had died, James recorded these wonders and much else besides in his own book.

# II

# The Book of James, Son of Joseph

And this is the testimony of James:

In the history of the twelve tribes of Israel is the story of a certain Joachim, a rich man, who used to offer twice as much as other pious men in the Temple: one portion for the good of the people, and one portion for his own sinfulness. When the Sabbath approached, Joachim was upbraided by Reuben the priest: "How is it that you, a rich man, favored by God in every other way, have no offspring? It is not lawful for you to make a show of your gifts when your name will die with you."

Joachim was grieved at Reuben's words, for he knew them to be true: All the righteous of Israel, from Abraham onward, had given children to Israel. And so Joachim left the Temple, ashamed to face his wife, and he went out into the desert where he fasted for forty days and nights. "I will never go home," he said to himself, "until the Lord answers my prayers, for his words are my meat and my drink."

Now Joachim's wife was named Anna. When Joachim did not return from the Temple she thought to herself, "My husband has deserted me, since I have given him no children." While she was weeping, two women came into the house. One, whose name was Rachel, wagged her finger at Anna: "You have made your husband a laughingstock in Israel. It's no wonder he left you. If the Lord had loved you, he would have granted you children. As it is, you will lead a life of torment and misery because your rivals for Joachim's love will call you Anna the 'Barren.' " And Rachel left the house, smiling at Anna's distress.

But the other woman, whose name was Judith, comforted her friend and sang to her:

> The Lord saves his daughters
> from the tongues of scolders,
> he saves us from the scorn of rivals:
> My heart rejoices in the Lord,
> it rejoices because of his mighty works.
> The strong are scattered by his arm,
> the weak become strong and do not falter;
> Those who had plenty bargain for scraps,
> and the hungry are satisfied:
> The barren woman has seven children,
> and the mother of many sons is left to languish.

But Anna wept, and stitched sackcloth to cover her body. Her cheeks were flushed from weeping, and dark circles ringed her eyes. No sadder song had ever been heard among the daughters of Judah:

> My mind is diseased, my days numbered;
> I pray to God for the earth to cover me;
> My days fade like an echo,
> Their brightness darkened by sneers;
> Morning light blackens before me
> My name a-whisper beneath the clatter of pots;
> My heart strings are snapped.

When the sabbath came and Judith found Anna still in mourning, she said to her, "See, I have brought you a present—a headband worthy of a queen. Take it and put it on: show yourself to the people. You have mourned long enough over Joachim and your childlessness."

But Anna cursed Judith, flung the headband away, and raised her hand to strike her: "Go away from this doorpost: the Lord has humbled me, even though I have done nothing. I am sinless and have no children. But you are the mother of seven and a sinner. There is guile in your gift. You and the others have done this to me. You have made a sinless woman a partaker in your sins. You have defiled my house and driven my husband away."

Judith took away the headband, and at the doorpost she said, "There is no need for me to curse this house. God has cursed it. He has shut up your womb like a grave so that your seed will rot and never be fruit in Israel."

Anna remained in her house for a fortnight, afraid to venture out, neglected by friends. One morning when she awoke she said to herself, "How long must I endure the reproaches of Israel? I will pray for an answer from the Lord." She stripped off her mourning garments, bathed, anointed her head, perfumed her body, and dressed herself in a bridal gown. At noon, she went to the garden to walk, and there she saw a laurel tree and sat down to pray.

"God of our fathers," she said, "Bless me as you blessed Sarah, to whom you gave a son, Isaac." She was startled at the sound of sparrows, high in the tree, as they chattered their praises to God, and her spirit sank. "Lord, I am not even as fruitful as the beasts of the earth, for they sing your praises, and the birds of the air are fruitful, according to your law. But me—I am a curse on the house of Israel. I am not even as fruitful as the streams that bear life and sing praise to you. I am a curse on the house of Judah. I am a worse creature than the clay, for the ground raises up fruit to God in its season and blesses the Lord. I am a curse on the house of Israel; I have no way to praise you, my God."

But an angel of the Lord stood just beside Anna and said, "Anna, Anna: Do you suppose the Lord has not heard you? You will conceive, and the fruit of your womb will be famous throughout the world."

Anna fell down before the angel, and trembling said to him: "Sir, I know that God my deliverer keeps his promises. No matter whether I bear a boy or a girl, I will give it back as a thank-offering to the Lord. It will devote its life to serving him and nothing else."

Just then, two messengers approached. Finding Anna in the garden, they told her wonders about Joachim her husband—how he had taken himself into the desert and prayed to God, and how God had sent an angel to him saying, "Joachim, Go home. Your wife, Anna, is pregnant with your seed." Joachim had leapt up and ordered his herdsmen to round up ten spotless lambs to be offered to God; twelve tender calves for the priests and assembly of elders, and a hundred kids for the people.

While the messengers were still speaking, Joachim himself was spotted on the road into the city with his flocks. Anna stood at the gate, and ran to him and embraced him. "Husband," she said, "what woman has been blessed as I have been blessed? For the widow is a widow no more, and the childless woman will bear fruit for Israel and for the Lord." Joachim and Anna went into the house and Joachim rested from his trials.

The next day at sunrise Joachim went to the Temple to make a thank-offering to the Lord. Reuben the priest met him at the gate of the Temple: "Do you think, " said Reuben, "that God will accept your offering? If you were righteous, God would have given you sons; as it is, God spurns your offerings and you are a laughingstock."

Joachim placed his offering on the plate and said to Reuben: "God has favored me. I have seen a vision of angels, and I know that the Lord has forgiven me my sins. Anna is pregnant with my seed."

Reuben considered what Joachim had said, and then replied, "If what you say is true, Joachim, that God has blessed you, then I find no fault in you either." And Joachim was counted from that day on among the righteous.

Time passed and on the 15th of Hathor, in her ninth month, Anna gave birth to a baby girl whom she named Miriam, and after purifying herself she nursed the baby and sang a song to the Lord in thanksgiving:

> My heart rejoices in the Lord,
>> in the Lord I now hold my head high;
>> my mouth is full of derision for my foes,
>> exultant because you have saved me.

Day by day, the little girl grew stronger. When Miriam was six months old, Anna stood her on the ground to see if she could stand. The baby ran seven steps, then ran back to her mother laughing. "I promise the Lord," said Anna, clutching the child, "that your feet will not touch the ground again before I have made good my vow to bring you to the Lord's Temple." In the meantime, Anna hallowed a space in the bedchamber and found seven of the most beautiful virgins in Israel to tend to the baby.

Nothing defiled or common was permitted near her.

At the end of a year Joachim provided a great feast for the priests and elders and invited everyone to witness the dedication of the child. The priests held her to heaven and spoke these words:

> By the living God
> the God of Abraham and Isaac,
> We dedicate the child Miriam
> To the service of his holy places.
> O God bless this child and give her
> A name to be revered for generations.

And the people shouted, "So be it! Amen!" Then the high priest blessed her forehead with oil and said, "Lord, God of the high places: look down on this child and bless her as you have blessed no one before her." Anna clutched at the child and took her to her breast to suck. Then she sang a song of thanksgiving:

> I will sing to the Lord
> >  to the Lord who has confounded my enemies;
> >  The Lord has given me a fruit of his righteousness
> >  The harvest of his vineyard through my womb:
> >  What son of Reuben will not know
> >  That Anna the barren has given suck?
> >  Listen, people of Judah: Anna the barren
> >  nurses her child!

When the feast had ended, the priests and elders, Anna's maids and Joachim's menservants left the house praising God and reveling in his wonders.

When Miriam was two years old, she was taken to the Temple to fulfill the promise Anna had made to God. But at the Temple gate Anna held back, looked at her only child and said, "Husband, she is very young. I am afraid that she will miss her father and mother and that her crying after us will be a distraction for the priests. Might it not be better to wait until the child is older?"

Now Joachim loved Miriam more than his life, but he knew a debt was owed to God. "Anna," he said, "We must pay God what is due on time: if we hold back, our gift will be required of us and then it is a gift no more." But when he saw Anna's tears, he relented: "Yes," he said, "Let us wait until she is three years old."

For a full year they delighted in Miriam's presence in the household. She was like no other child among the daughters of Israel, for she could play the harp and sing psalms. She had surpassed her

55

mother at sewing and embroidery, and everything she did was perfectly done. Her radiance brightened her father's heart and she was her mother's joy. But when the child was three, Joachim said to Anna, "The time is right. We must take her to the priests and pay God his due. Call seven daughters of Israel, being certain they are pure, and ask them to light lamps and to keep them burning so that Miriam's heart will not be turned away from serving God."

This time, Anna did not quarrel; she knew that the promise was owed to God and that a gift delayed is no gift. And so the lamps were lit as a symbol and seal of the promise, and Miriam was taken to the Temple of the Lord. There, the high priest received her and kissed her, anointed her forehead and blessed her with a prophecy:

> The Lord will make your name great,
>> greater than that of any daughter of Eve:
>> Through you, the Lord will accomplish
>> the redemption of Israel and of all people.

Then Reuben instructed her to sit on the third step of the altar. The grace of God was in her, and she danced on the third step and sang psalms to God. All the priests, and the whole house of Israel loved her, and it was said of her, "She is Anna's child, the daughter of Joachim. She is the dove of the Temple and the delight of everyone. But she takes food from no man: she is fed by the hand of an angel."

# III

# The History of the Virgin

And Mary said to James, "When I was a child, I was promised by my mother, Anna, to God. My father's name was Joachim, and he was of the tribe of Judah and of David's stock. I was born in the village of Magdalia,[1] sometimes being known as Mary of Cleopas and other times as your mother, as Mary of James, the son of Joseph."

"And what of your grandparents?" asked James. "My grandfather was a rich and devout man named David, who was visited by an angel. He was told that the messiah would come through his seed. His wife's name was Sarah, and she bore him a son, my father, Joachim. My mother is from the family of Aminidab, who was David's brother."

James sat very close to Mary, eager to hear the story of her life in the Temple. And this is what he recorded:

When Mary got to be twelve years old, the priests held a council to decide what should be done. It was forbidden for a girl of child-bearing age to sit in the sanctuary of the Lord. Finally, the high priest said, "I will go up to the altar of the Lord and I will pray for guidance. We must do what God reveals we should do." And the high priest took the holy vestment with the twelve bells, one for each of the tribes of Israel and he entered the Holy of Holies, and covering his face he prayed to the Lord. A man of light stood beside him and said, "Zecharias, go out and assemble all of the widowers in the city: you must ask them to bring their staffs with them. The Lord will make a sign of the staff of the man he chooses to be the husband of Mary."

Zecharias ran to tell the priests of the wonder. "My brothers," he said, "command the heralds and horns to announce the word of the Lord, for he spoke to me in the Holy of Holies. And tell all the men who are widowers to bring their staffs so that the Lord can work his sign." So the horns were sounded and the messengers went out of the Temple. Soon all the widowers in Jerusalem had assembled.

Joseph had been working in his shop, but when he heard the sound of the horn he threw down his adze and ran to meet the high priest, holding his staff in his right hand. The high priest collected the staffs and took them into the Temple where he prayed for the sign. But the staffs were unchanged. The priest prayed again, but still no sign appeared. And so the priest took the staffs and returned them to their owners, and Joseph was the last to receive his staff. Suddenly, a dove emerged from the tip of the rod and it flew first toward heaven, then swooped and perched atop Joseph's head. The priest was astonished and the widowers of Israel marveled at the sign. Then Zecharias spoke: "God has spoken his word. The lot has fallen to you, Joseph: take the girl from the Temple as your wife."

But Joseph refused. "I have been married already. I have sons and daughters older than this girl. The sons of Israel will laugh at an old man like me taking one so young as his wife."

When Zechariah heard Joseph, he bristled. "Joseph, have you

no fear of your God? Do you forget what terrible things God did to Dathan, Abiram, and Korah[2] when they denied him—how the earth split and swallowed them up? Do you want to risk the ruin of your house?"

Joseph was afraid. So he took the girl by the hand and said, "Come, Mary: I take you for safekeeping from the Temple of my God. You will bide in my house where angels shall watch over you. But it would be a scandal for me to bed you, and so I will keep myself apart and, as much as possible, out of the house. I am a carpenter with buildings to build and my work will keep me away."

Now about this time the priests had decided to make a veil for the Temple of the Lord. The veil would be richly decorated, of pure silk, with hyacinthine, gold, scarlet, and true purple. Only one of the undefiled daughters of Israel would be permitted to weave the veil, and the priests remembered, above all others, Mary the virgin who had been given to Joseph for a wife. And so the guard of the Temple went round the city and brought back seven virgins, among them Mary, and the high priest said, "Cast lots so that we can decide which of you will weave the veil." The lot fell to Mary and the priest handed over to her the silk, the gold, the hyacinthine, the scarlet, and the true purple, and Mary took them with her to Joseph's house.

And so, while Joseph was away, Mary sat by the window of the house and holy doves ministered to her needs. All day she would sit and work at her handicraft, singing the praises of God, her voice so sweet, so clear, so holy that the birds would light on her windowsill and cock their heads at the sound, for they loved to hear her singing.

# IV

# The Annunciation

It was around the time that Mary was at work on the Temple veil that Zechariah, the high priest, was struck dumb. (This was when Herod was prince in Judaea.) Elizabeth, his wife, of the house of Aaron, a kinswoman of Mary, was barren and had no hope of having children for Israel since she was enfeebled by the years and her husband had lost his appetite for her. One day, however, when Zechariah was performing his priestly duties, burning incense in the Temple, a day when many people had gathered at the Temple for prayer, a man of light stood next to the old priest, just to the right side of the altar of incense.

Zechariah fell to his knees in terror, but the angel told him to brace himself: "Your wife, Elizabeth, is to have a child whose name you will call John. He will be the apple of your eye, the delight of your old age, and many will rejoice at his birth. John will be great in the eyes of the Lord: he will live like a hermit, filled with God's spirit from his mother's womb, and because of him many children of Israel will turn to God. Like Elijah, he will have the power to turn the fathers' hearts around. He will turn the disobedient back to the Law, and he will prepare the people for the coming of the Lord's anointed."

Zechariah trembled and said to the angel, "What you say may be true, but how can I know for certain: I am an old man, and my wife is an old woman, well beyond having children."

With this the angel seemed to give off a terrible radiance, and he said to Zechariah: "Don't you know me? I am Gabrhi-el, the one who stands next to the throne of God. I am sent to announce what God has in store for you. But because you have doubted, you will be struck speechless until everything I have said has happened!"

The people in the outer court of the Temple wondered about Zechariah, for he remained with the angel a very long time. But when he came out he could not speak. He waved his hands in the direction of the altar of incense and raised them to heaven, so that the people understood that the old man had seen a vision.

When he arrived home in the evening, Elizabeth greeted him at the door. "Husband," she said, "I am pregnant with your seed and in my fifth month." Zechariah embraced his wife, knowing that the word of the Lord had come to him and that God's plan was unfolding just as the angel had said. But Zechariah could say nothing, for he was still speechless from his disbelief.

In the sixth month of Elizabeth's pregnancy, the man of light whose name is Gabrhi-el was sent to the house of Joseph in Galilee, to the virgin Mary. Mary was at work spinning the scarlet and true purple for the decoration of the Temple veil, and being thirsty she took a jar and went outside the house to fetch water from the well. She heard a voice saying,

> Mary: you are highly favored by God,
> blessed above all women,
> full of God's grace.

Mary looked to her right, then to her left to see where the voice came from, but she saw nothing. Trembling with fear, she went into the house, put the jar on a stand, and began to measure the purple thread. Her eyes were cast to the floor, but she sensed before her a radiant presence and when she looked up a man of light was standing in front of her. "Don't be afraid, Mary. God favors you. You will conceive his very Word."

But Mary could not grasp the angel's greeting, and so she said, "It is not possible for a woman who has not slept with a man to conceive. Am I to suppose that I will give birth to the Word of the living God in the natural way?"

"No," said Gabrhi-el, "The power of God's spirit shall come upon you, the power of the most high God will overwhelm you. The holy thing which you will conceive will be called the Son of God. But you will call him by the name 'Jesus,' for this boy will save the people from sin."

"But how can this be possible," Mary said.

And the angel replied, "It is possible because with God everything is possible. Remember your cousin Elizabeth, who was a laughingstock because she had given her husband no children: Elizabeth is in the sixth month of her pregnancy."

Mary knelt before the angel, whose radiance now filled the room, and submitted to him: "I am God's maiden to do with as he chooses: let it happen as you have said."

When Mary had finished with the decoration of the veil, she brought her work to the Temple and the priests marveled at the beauty of her craft. Samuel the priest blessed her and said, "Mary, not only for this but for greater things God has magnified your name. You will be remembered throughout all generations."

And Mary sang in the Temple.

# V

# The Visit and Trial

Now Mary went to the house of Elizabeth her cousin and she knocked at the door. Elizabeth put down her wool, ran to the door, and found Mary standing outside. "Bless you, kinswoman," she said to her, "But how is it that the mother of my Lord should come to visit me?" And Elizabeth told Mary that the babe in her womb had leaped for joy, and she said to her, "Mary, you are the most favored of women, for your son is the child of the most high God."

But Mary shuddered at the message of the angel Gabrhi-el and looked to heaven and begged God to forget her: "Who am I to be chosen as the mother of my Lord? I am not worthy even to pronounce the holy name; how am I supposed to bear the Word?"

And Mary shared with Elizabeth the story of the angel's visitation; then she said, "But I dare not go back to Joseph. He will never believe me."

Elizabeth comforted Mary, and Mary for her part remained three months in the house of Zechariah, who had been struck dumb by God for his unbelief.

\*　　\*　　\*

Day by day, Mary's pregnancy advanced. Now she was sixteen years old when the mystery began, and she was afraid to show herself to Joseph, so she hid herself from the children of Israel, knowing they would stone her if her pregnancy came to light. At last, in Mary's sixth month, Elizabeth insisted that the girl go to her own house to wait for Joseph. "He is a righteous man in the eyes of God; God will give him a sign to open his heart to you." And Mary left Elizabeth's house and returned to Nazareth in Galilee to await Joseph's home-coming.

Joseph came home from his work in a neighboring village. When he entered the house he saw Mary in the shadows, her belly swollen. And Joseph grasped at his beard, threw himself on the floor, and beat the ground like a man possessed. He wept bitterly and tore at his shirt. Then, in a fit, he cried out to heaven:

> I cannot look my God in the face.
>> I cannot find the words to tell my grief.
>> I took this girl from the Temple, a virgin,
>> and now: see her. Who has done this thing to me?
>> Who has defiled the girl in my house?
>> Lord, is not the tale of Adam retold in me?
>> For it was while Adam slept that the serpent
>> had his way and seduced Eve, and it has happened
>> here in just the same way.

Joseph turned to Mary, and he said in anger: "Woman: God cared for you. How is it that you repay him in deceit? You were raised on the food of angels, nourished by the hand of God—and now you make me and my family eat the dirt of the road."

Joseph turned his back on the girl while she wept. And she said to him, "Man: I have not betrayed you. I have been faithful to the promises of God and my promise to you. I am innocent—I have never been with a man."

But Joseph would not hear her. His heart was like stone at that moment, like the flint used for sickles: "There is a baby in your belly: it did not come from nowhere."

But Mary pleaded with him until the stone of his heart became like clay, like wax at the sound of her words. When she had finished, Joseph left her and thought for a long time about what to do with the girl: "If I hide her sin, I am a sinner myself. The law of God requires me to expose her. But if she is telling the truth, if the seed in her is from an angel and I expose her to the sons of Israel, they will destroy her and I will have innocent blood on my hands."

Joseph weighed the choice until evening and decided finally to send her away quietly. Among a foreign people she might conceal her sin. Then he would not be guilty of her blood. With raised hands he prayed,

> I have had no dealings with falsehood
>> and have never deceived a son of Israel:
>> I have checked my eyes
>> never to take notice of the girl:
>> Let God weigh me on true scales
>> and he will know I am innocent!
>> And if I am found a sinner,
>> If I have looked wrongfully at her,
>> If there is dirt on my hands,
>> May another eat what I sow.
>> If my heart has wanted her
>> And I am being punished for my desire,
>> Then let other men take her for a slave.

When night came Joseph lay himself down outside the house and had a vision of an angel. The angel stood near him and called him by name, "Joseph. Don't be afraid of this child. It comes from the power of the spirit which has overwhelmed Mary, your wife. It is not the seed of any man which has done this. Mary will have a son, and you will name him Jesus, for he will be the one who saves his people."

When Joseph awoke he praised God and went into the house where Mary was sitting at the window. And Joseph watched over her, day and night, neglecting everything to protect her.

In time his absence from the Temple was noticed and a teacher named Annas came to his doorpost and called his name. "Joseph," he said, "we have missed you in the congregation."

Warily, Joseph made his excuses. "I am weary from travel and need to be at home for a while."

But Annas was subtle, and as Joseph was speaking he peered through the window of the bedchamber and saw Mary, her belly swollen. Annas wasted no time. He hurried to the priest and said, "Sir, I know that Joseph the carpenter is highly regarded but I must report that he is guilty of a terrible sin."

The priest, who counted Joseph a righteous man, was troubled: "And why do you bring this accusation?" he said.

"Because," replied Annas, "he has not kept Mary safe, the girl who was given to his charge from the Temple. She is pregnant. Furthermore, Joseph has concealed her guilt and has made himself a sinner in not exposing her to the sons of Israel for judgment."

So Annas was instructed by the priest to fetch Mary and Joseph and bring them before him at the judgment seat. The priest took his place and looked first at Mary: "You, my girl, were raised in the Temple. Day and night you were near the Holy of Holies. You were nurtured by angels and danced and sang the praises of God at the altar. Is this not so?"

And Mary answered, "Yes. But I am guilty of nothing. By the living God I am pure. Neither Joseph nor any man has touched me."

The priest was silent for a moment, and then turned his gaze on

Joseph. "You have let this happen. And having seen it, you did not expose her guilt to the sons of Israel."

But Joseph said, "I have done nothing wrong. I know only that I cannot restore her to the Temple." And he held his tongue from saying anything further.

The priest rose from the judgment seat and looked first at Mary, then at Joseph. "You are sinners together," he said. "And you have lied to me before the face of God." And he commanded an officer to bring the water of bitterness.[1]

Then before the people, he made Joseph drink from the cup. And Joseph did so, and wandered in the hill country for a few days, but he returned to the priest as spry as before. Then Mary was ordered to drink, and she did. And like Joseph, she returned from wandering in the hill country as healthy as she was before she had drunk the stinking water. The people were astonished, and the priest no less so. "If God has chosen not to make your sin manifest," he said, "I cannot condemn you."

And Mary and Joseph returned from the place of judgment glorifying God for the wonder he had performed.

# VI

# The Nativity of John

It was about this time that Elizabeth gave birth to the son promised to her by God. And when her friends and neighbors heard the news of the birth they were as delighted as she was. In accordance with the law, when the eighth day came they took the child to be circumcised and at his presentation those present named him "Zechariah," after his father. But Elizabeth spoke up and said, "No, he is not to be called Zechariah but *John*."

The people were astounded. "Woman: there is no one in your family with a name like that." And so they looked to Zechariah for some sign of his wishes in the matter, since the old man still had no power to speak. And Zechariah took a tablet of clay and wrote in Hebrew this sentence: "His name is John."

As soon as he had done this, his tongue was freed and his lips began to move. And he praised God for the marvel that had happened to him, while all the people looked on in amazement. Everyone who witnessed these things began to spread the news that something wonderful was taking place, and all over Judaea the story of

John's birth became the common talk. All the villagers began to wonder, "What will this child become, for surely the hand of the Lord is upon him."

Zechariah spoke this prophecy:
 Praise the God of Israel:
 God has visited and redeemed his people.
 He has raised a horn of salvation for us,
 his servants in the House of Israel.
 He has spoken by the mouths of holy prophets
 since the world began
 that we would find salvation from our enemies
 and from those that hate us,
 that he would deal kindly with our fathers
 who kept the holy covenant.

This was the oath he swore to Abraham our father,
 that he would save us from the hands of the enemy
 and give us the power to worship him without fear,
 with a holy heart, in holy worship
 in his presence, as long as we should live.
 You, my child, will be called Prophet,
 servant of the high God, Preparer of the Lord's way,
 And you will lead the people to safety
 through the knowledge of him
 and by the forgiveness of their sins.
 In the mercy of our God,
 the morning star, the sun of righteousness
 has risen in our sky, to shine on those
 who live in darkness, in death's shadow,
 and to guide our feet safely along the path.

John grew strong in mind and body, and was under the protection of his father and mother until he took himself into the desert as a sign.

# VII

# The Nativity of Jesus, Called the Christ

In the ninth month of Mary's pregnancy, the emperor Augustus ordered a census of Judaean villages. Now Joseph's stock came from Bethlehem, a city of David, and Joseph made preparations to record himself and his family on the census rolls. But as he prepared, he wondered to himself, "I can record my sons—but what shall I do with this girl? Am I to record her as my wife? No, I am ashamed of her. As my daughter? But everyone knows she is not my daughter." And he sighed deeply, "Ah, I shall leave it to God. Let him guide my hand in the matter."

So Joseph saddled the donkey and set Mary upon it. And James led it out of the village, with Joseph following behind. When they were about three miles from Bethlehem Joseph saw Mary in the throes of labor, and he walked alongside her and saw the pain in her face. But then, as suddenly as it had come, the pain left her and he saw her laughing. "Mary," he said, "what is the matter with you? I see you in pain at one moment, laughing the next."

And Mary said, "Husband, it is because I see two nations before my face: the one weeping and lamenting, the other rejoicing and laughing."[1]

They were still well outside the city when Mary said, "Joseph, get me down quickly. The babe in my womb presses to come out."

And Joseph took her down, but could find only a cave to shelter the family for the night. "We will hide your shame outside the city," he said, "for this place is a desert."

James and the other sons of Joseph stood close beside Mary while Joseph set out toward the city to find a midwife. James heard these things years beyond from his father, and this is his testimony, the words of his father, Joseph, in recalling the wonders.

# VIII

# The Testimony of Joseph the Carpenter to the Night of Wonders

Now I, Joseph, was walking along toward the village of Bethlehem in order to procure a midwife. But then, all of a sudden, I was not walking; I stood still with my feet still astride. In amazement I looked to the heavens—it was as though the very air were motionless—and the heavens were frozen. The birds in the sky did not move against the vault of the heavens.

I cast my eyes down to the earth, where just beside me some shepherds had been having their supper, the platters spread out in front of them. But not one of them moved: their mouths were open, as if to chew or to eat. But they lay like wood, neither chewing nor eating and with their eyes cast upward to the heavens.

Some sheep were being herded just ahead of me, but in that instant they stood still, and the shepherd, seeing them stop, had raised his staff to drive them on, but he too was fixed in his course. Goats were lapping water from the stream that ran along beside me, but they were caught in a flash with their tongues touching water that had become like glass.

And as suddenly as it had happened, things began once again to move. Voices rang out in the still air; the birds soared and swooped; the workers took their food and the shepherd cursed his flocks. The kids drank their fill from the swirls of the stream.

About that time I saw a woman on the road ahead of me and just as she might have passed by me she took me by the arm and said,

"Man: where are you heading?"

"I must find a midwife in Bethlehem," I answered.

"And are you a Jew?"

"Yes," I said and made ready to get by her.

But the woman persisted. "Who is it who's giving birth in a cave, then?"

"Woman," I said, "it is none of your business, but she happens to be my betrothed wife, Mary."

"I see," said the woman. "Then she is not your wife?"

"She is Mary, who was reared in the Temple and she was given to me by lot when God worked a wonder among the widowers of Israel. She is my betrothed wife, and the child she is bearing is in her by the power of the holy spirit."

"Now I have heard everything," said the woman, "but you are in luck, as I am a midwife myself, Zelomi by name. Seeing is believing. I will go with you to see." And the midwife went with me.

(Here ends the transcript of Joseph, given to his son James, also known as James the Just.)

# IX

# The Midwife's Account of the Nativity

These are the wonders I saw on the night when the savior of the world was born to Mary the virgin. First, she cast her eyes toward heaven and became as white as snow in the presence of the light from above. The birth of the Lord was like light passing through thin glass: first showing dimly from her, and then filling the cave with its brightness. Everything around the child shined with the beauty of the sun: it was wonderful to see it! And Mary worshiped the child that had come from her.

I felt that his warmth was peace and that every moment peace was growing on the earth. And as I was watching the wonders, a thousand angel voices seemed to explode in the night air: *"Amen!"* they said, and the light flashed and the cave was filled with brightness and a sweet aroma. How shall I describe it? His birth was like the rising of the sun, like the dew that descends in the morning when it touches the fields with its sweetness.

But once the light had flashed, the brightness began to fade, and in a while the child looked like a natural child—like any baby—as the light withdrew. Ah, but he was not like others. For when my fear left me, I reached down to touch him and to hold him, but when I lifted him I remarked that it was like lifting a flower, almost without weight. And while other children are gnarled and ugly at birth, this child had no ugliness about him. He was all shining and beautiful, as though God had shaped him to delight our eyes. And whilst most babies whine and cry and worry their mothers, this baby made no sound at all. Instead, as I held him he looked square at me and smiled sweetly; and suddenly his eyes flashed like lightning from the mountains, and I worshiped him.

And I stayed to see still more marvels. When Joseph led Mary from the cave after a spell, they went into a stable and she laid her child in a manger meant for the animals. The ox and the ass knelt down and worshiped him, as the elders used to say, "The ox knows his owner and the ass knows his master's crib." And again, "You are found between the beasts." And Joseph did not leave the woman's side.

Joseph and I approached the cave, but we could see nothing within it because a blinding bright cloud rose just in front of the entrance. "I am truly blessed this night," said I. "I have seen with my own eyes the wonder of God and the salvation of Israel." And just as I said this, the cloud became a mist and disappeared into thin air.

But the light entered the cave and grew brighter, so intense that no mortal could endure its radiance. Joseph and myself, we covered our faces in fear; then, little by little, the light grew dim, and when we uncovered our faces and looked ahead, we saw a newborn baby sucking at Mary's breast.

I ran from the cave singing the praises of God for the wonder, and outside I found Salome who had seen the light from a distance. "Salome! Salome," said I, "I have seen unbelievable wonders. The man Joseph has told me that his espoused wife Mary, a virgin of Israel, was bearing the seed of God's holy spirit. And this night the son of God has been born to a virgin!"

Salome scoffed at the notion, and pushed her way past me say-ing, "Woman, you will believe any tale. What man would not want you to think better of him than someone who has violated a virgin of Israel, and now tries to conceal his guilt out here—in a hole in the wilderness."

Salome entered the cave, me on her heels, and I said to Mary, "Lift your skirt. The woman named Salome wants to see if you are still tight."

And Mary did as she was asked. Salome's fingers groped to make the test, but with each prod they burned, and when she with-drew her hand it was aflame and fell from her wrist leaving only a stump at the end of her arm.

Salome shrieked and fell to her knees, and made this prayer to God for her unbelief:

> Oh, God of my fathers,
>> You are the God of Abraham, Isaac, and Jacob,
>> And I am a daughter of Israel.
>> Do not humiliate me in front of the people.
>> Do not take my hand from doing your work
>> Among the poor. When I was whole,
>> I was your servant, and I performed
>> Cures in your name.

Then, a man of light stood next to her in the cave, and he said to her, "Salome, your prayer has been heard. Take the baby from its mother, cradle it in your afflicted arm. He is your salvation and joy."

And Salome did as she was told. She took the baby and looked tenderly at his face, and raising her eyes she said, "Our redeemer lives. This child is our king and I worship him."

As soon as she had said this, Salome's hand was restored. She ran from the cave intending to spread the news around the coun-tryside, but the voice of the angel came from heaven: "Salome, say nothing about what you have seen—do not even whisper these marvels until the child enters Jerusalem."

After three days, Joseph led James and Mary, with the baby at her breast, to a stable near to the gate of the city of Bethlehem. There she swaddled him and Joseph made a bed of the hay in a feeding trough while the animals looked on. And Mary took the child and lay him in the manger and sang sweetly to him through the night.

After a time, the news of the wonder was given to some shepherds who were driving their flocks across the hills. As it was quite late, and they had drunk their fill, they made themselves comfortable for the night. Just then, a light appeared above them and grew brighter and brighter, until they were startled from their snoring. When they awoke they were blinded and could hear only a voice:

> Get up, and go toward Bethlehem,
> the city of David.
> A child has been born,
> a messiah and savior, the Lord himself.
> You will find him in a stable,
> swaddled and lying in a feeding trough for the animals.

And just as suddenly as the voice had sounded, a thousand angels filled the skies and sang a psalm to God:

> Glorious is the High God!
> Glorious is the peace of God!
> Glorious is the mercy he shows to his creatures.

And then the sky darkened and the angels were gone. The shepherds raised themselves from the ground in confusion. "It has been nearly three days since we saw the light in the cave and since nature stopped in her tracks. Let's do as we are told and not think we're seeing things." And so the shepherds moved toward Bethlehem.

Just as the angel had promised, they found a stable, full of light, and inside they found the child, asleep in a manger, with Mary kneeling close beside him and Joseph keeping watch. And they saw in these happenings the fulfillment of the words of the prophet Habakkuk:

> The holy one comes,
> his radiance overspreads the skies,
> and his splendor fills the earth.
> He rises like the dawn,
> with twin rays starting forth at his side;
> the skies are the hiding place of his majesty,
> and the everlasting ways are for his swift flight.

And as other prophets had foretold, the ox and the ass swayed before him in adoration. The shepherds remained for three days, praising God. When they left the stable, they ran into the city and began to spread the news of the child's birth. But no one who heard their story believed them, and so they returned to the stable to see it all again for themselves, but they found the animals eating from the manger, the woman and her child gone.

# X

# The Circumcision

On the sixth day after the birth of Jesus, Joseph took Mary and the child at her breast into the city of Bethlehem to keep the sabbath and they remained in the city until the eighth day when the boy was taken and circumcised by the priest. (This was according to the law of Moses, which declares that every male that is born to a woman is holy in the eyes of God.) And when the week of her purification was ended, Joseph brought the boy to the Temple in order to dedicate him to the Lord and to perform the rituals commanded by the law. So he took two turtle doves and gave them to the priest for sacrifice.

Now living in the vicinity of the Temple was a man named Simeon who was famous for his piety. Day by day he sat in the court of the Temple hoping for some sign of the Messiah. God had promised him that death would not touch him before he had looked on the face of the Christ. And so, according to his custom, he came to the Temple at midday and he saw Joseph and Mary and the baby in her arms. Simeon was filled with the spirit of God, and ran to take the boy from its mother's arms.

Cradling it, he lifted his eyes to heaven and sang:

> Now, Lord, let your servant depart peacefully,
>> according to your holy word;
>> for I have seen with my eyes your salvation,
>> the salvation which is spread before all people:
>> a light to give hope to the gentiles,
>> but the glory of your people Israel.

Joseph wondered at what Simeon had said, but Mary kept everything close to her heart. Simeon then blessed them both and said to Mary very sternly: "Woman, this child is a sign—a sign over which many in Israel will stumble, a sign of the life and salvation of the people, but a sign which many will reject. And do not think that your lot will be easy. A sword will pierce your heart so that the thoughts of the people might be known."

And when Simeon had uttered his prophecy, a woman named Anna, known to be a prophetess, came forward. Anna was eighty-four years old and had remained a virgin for seven years beyond her marriage. She was the daughter of a certain Phanuel of the tribe of Asher, and she roamed the Temple precinct day and night, begging for crumbs, fasting and praying. And when Anna saw Mary, she praised God and went round the Temple saying, "See, here: this is the one who will redeem Israel. The Christ has come to Jerusalem. Our redeemer lives! I have seen him with my own eyes."

And Joseph and Mary performed all of the things essential to the law of Moses, and made plans to return to Bethlehem.

# XI

## The Jealousy of a King

As Joseph prepared to go to Bethlehem, rumor spread as far as Jerusalem that Herod the prince was in a rage. Diviners from the east had visited him and they had said, "We have seen a sign in the heavens that a new king has arisen over the Jews, and we have come to pay him homage. Be good enough to show us where he is."

But Herod had heard of no such thing, and so, after extending the hospitality of his house to the magi, he sent his spies to them and called for the high priest. "Tell me," he said to the priest "what is written about the messiah who will rule over Israel—where is he to be born?"

And the priest replied, "It is written that he will be born in Judaea, in the town of Bethlehem."

Herod then said to the magi, "Tell me, you have seen a sign: what sort of sign?"

And the magi said, "We have seen a great star, a star so radiant that the other stars could not be seen. From this we knew that a king had been born to rule over the Jews, and we have come to worship him."

Herod decided not to press them further, but sent them on their way, with instructions that when they found the child they should make his whereabouts known so that he might worship him as well.

The magi went out of Jerusalem and followed the star, and they followed it for two years until it came to rest over a cave. Entering the place, they saw the young child and Mary its mother and they unpacked their gifts: gold, incense, and resin. But as they prepared to leave, an angel appeared to them and warned them not to return to Herod, since he was out to murder the child. And so, they returned to their provinces by a different route, glorifying God.

When Herod discovered that he had been tricked by the magi, he paid murderers to scour the countryside and ordered them to kill all children two years and under. And when Mary heard that Herod was in a rage, she decided to disguise the young child; and so, she took him and wrapped him in swaddling clothes and hid him in an ox-manger.[1]

Meantime, Elizabeth had heard of Herod's process against the infants, and fearing for John's life, she took the boy to the hills and looked around for a place to hide him. But Elizabeth was old and feeble, and she could not get up into the mountains. So she raised her eyes to heaven and she cried, "Mountains of God: Have mercy on a mother and her only child!" And immediately the mountain split in two and swallowed her and the infant John, and within it stood a man of light who watched and protected them.

Now Herod recalled that Zechariah had been a given a son in his old age and that Elizabeth had been a laughingstock in Israel before God worked his wonder in her. So Herod sent a guard to kill the child, thinking that he might be the one whose star had appeared in the heavens.

The guards seized the old priest and demanded to know where he had hidden the infant John. But Zechariah, unaware that Eliza-

beth had fled with the boy to find a safe place, could only say,
"Leave me in peace. I am an old man, a priest who serves God, and
I cannot tell you where the boy is, nor his mother."

When the guards took this report to Herod, the king was enraged, and said, "The old man is lying. Now I know for certain that
his son is the one who will be the king of Israel," and he sent guards
again, this time to the Temple where Zechariah was walking in the
outer court, to deliver the following message:

"Know that your life is under my hand and that I have the power
to slay you or to let you breathe."

But Zechariah faced them squarely: "Shed my blood and I shall
be a martyr to the word of God. My spirit will fly to God because I
am innocent, and because you slay me in the forecourt of God's
Temple."

Laughing at the old man's words, the guards killed Zechariah
where he stood, just as the sun was coming up.

Now the guards had done this by stealth and no one entering the
Temple suspected that Zechariah had been slain. In time, however, the
people began to grumble: "Where is the old priest? He is usually
here to greet us when we arrive." And the priests too were worried that
Zechariah did not appear—until, afraid that something foul had happened, one of them went into the Temple and saw lying beside the altar
of incense Zechariah's body, a pool of blood congealed beside him.

And a voice spoke to the priest: "Zechariah has been slain, and
his blood cannot be wiped away until his death is repaid." The
priest, when he heard the voice, ran away terrified and told the others who waited outside for news.

Then the whole assembly of priests entered. The panels of the
Temple were split and the walls began to howl. They tore their
garments in half, for the altar of the Lord had been defiled. But
they could not find Zechariah's body, and the congealed blood
had turned to stone.

Fearing for themselves, the priests left the Temple and spread the news throughout Jerusalem that Zechariah had been murdered by Herod's men. And when the people heard the news they wailed for him for three days and nights. At the end of the third day the priests met in assembly to choose another to take Zechariah's place, and they chose Simeon, who was full of the spirit.

I, James the Just, son of Joseph the Carpenter, wrote these things in Jerusalem during the recent troubles, wherein Herod died.[2] And I hid myself in the wilderness until Jerusalem was again at peace. And I glorify God for granting me the wisdom to write this history. (Grace to those who love our Lord Jesus Christ: glory be to him for ever).

*Here end the accounts of James the Just.*[3]

# XII

# The Child Jesus in Egypt

When the Lord Jesus was two years old, diviners came from the east to worship him: Melkon of Persia, Gaspar of India, and Baalthazar of Arabia. But because of Herod's killing of the infants, Joseph was kept from returning to Judaea by an angel who said, "Take the child and its mother and go down into Egypt, so that the prophecy can be fulfilled: 'Out of Egypt I will call my son.' " And Joseph did what he was told.

On the way, Joseph and Mary and the child passed through a desert area infested with robbers. And fearing for the safety of his family, Joseph said: "Let us rest for a while and then move through the region at night when no one will spot us."

But just as he said this, two robbers spied the family at a distance. Their names were Titus and Dumachus and sleeping alongside the road not far from them was a band of twenty robbers. Titus saw Mary and had pity on her and said to his comrade, "Look: the woman is tired from her journey and she holds a young child. Let's keep their passing a secret and not wake the others. I will give you forty *drachmae* if you agree."

But Dumachus would not agree until he held Titus' purse in his hand. Then both of the robbers held their tongues and the others did not stir from their sleep.

Seeing that the two thieves had done her a good turn, Mary blessed them and said, "May God uphold you with his right hand, and may he forgive you your sins."

And looking up at his mother the Lord Jesus answered her: "Mother, in thirty years' time I will be crucified in Jerusalem and these two will be crucified alongside me: Titus on my right, Dumachus on my left. And Titus will enter Paradise ahead of me."

"Hush, child," Mary said to him. "God save you from such a fate."

And the family went its way, passing along beside a city famous for its idols. But as they passed, the city and all its inhabitants were changed into sandhills.

And they came to a sycamore tree near the place today called Matarea. And when Jesus was placed upon the ground to walk, a spring of fresh water gushed forth where his foot had made its imprint in the sand. Mary washed the child's shirt in the water, and from the sweat she wrung from it in that place the balsam tree appeared.

Finally, they came to a cave and got down to rest. But they were warned by some boys who were playing nearby that it was infested with huge serpents.[1] Just as they turned to go their way, the serpents flared from the mouth of the cave and the boys fled in terror. But Jesus got down from his mother's lap and faced the dragons. He lifted his hand as if to command them and they cowered in fear before him, and then retreated into the cave. This fulfilled the prophecy "Praise the Lord, you dragons from the earth, you dragons and all depths." But Jesus pursued the serpents, instructing them never to harm anyone, and Mary and Joseph went after the boy, afraid that he would be eaten alive. Seeing their concern, the child said, "Do not be afraid: all creatures must be quiet before me."

And so the lions and leopards worshiped Jesus and followed the family through the desert, going wherever they went. And the lions and leopards guided them through the wilderness with heads bent worshipfully, showing their obedience to God by wagging their tails and keeping to a reverent pace. When they came too close to Mary, Jesus would comfort her, saying with a radiant smile, "Don't worry, mother. They are not meant for harm but for help." And with words like this from his tiny lips he removed the fear from her heart.

With the lions marched oxen and asses and various beasts. And the lions and leopards mingled with the sheep and rams which Joseph had brought with him from Judaea, and the lions nuzzled the lambs affectionately, never doing harm. This was to fulfill the words of the prophet, "Good faith is his protection: the wolf will live with the sheep, the leopard will lie down with the kid, the calf and the young lion shall grow up together, and a little child shall lead them."

On the third day of their journey across the desert Mary was overcome by the heat of the sun and she said to Joseph, "Husband, I need to rest for a while beneath this palm tree."

Joseph obliged her, and led her to the palm tree and helped her dismount. Looking up, she saw the palm tree was laden with fruit and told Joseph that she craved it. But Joseph shrugged. "Woman: look at the size of this tree. It's no good asking me to get it for you. I might break my neck. Besides, we are three days out and our skins are nearly empty of water. If I were you, I wouldn't worry over fruit when our animals are thirsty."

But the child Jesus heard his mother's request and felt sorry for her. And he said to the palm, "Here: bend down and offer my mother some of your fruit." And as soon as he had said it the palm tree bowed itself down to Mary's feet. And quickly they gathered from the tree all the fruit they wanted.

But when they had finished, the palm tree was still bowed before them, as if waiting for the word of the child. So Jesus said, "Stand up straight and be strong like the trees that stand in Paradise where my father is. And open from your roots a stream of water: my mother and father are thirsty, and the animals need water."

And at the child's command, the tree stood up straight and the earth opened around its roots, and from it clear, sweet water appeared. Joseph and Mary were amazed at this, but drank their fill and then watered the animals.

When they were ready to leave, Jesus turned once more to the palm tree and spoke to it: "This palm does the will of the creator. And for that I grant it a privilege: that an angel will carry one of its branches to be planted in heaven. And when anyone has been recorded as righteous in the doing of my father's will, that person will be said to have won 'the palm of victory.' " And just as he had commanded, an angel of the Lord flew down from heaven and plucked a branch from the palm and carried it away to heaven.

When Mary and Joseph saw this they fell to the ground in fear. And Jesus smiled and said to them, "This palm was our salvation in the wilderness: now it will stand in the heavenly places as a sign of hope for all the blessed."

And they ventured on through the desert, until at last Joseph said, "We are burning in this heat. Let us cross over and make our way through the coastal towns and take advantage of the sea breezes."

And Jesus said, "Father, don't be afraid. I will make a month's journey last a day," and as he spoke the mountains and cities of Egypt, which by Joseph's calculations had been thirty days' journey, appeared in the distance.

So the family came to the city called Hermopolis Sotinen, famous among Egyptians as the place where a temple called the Capitol had been built during Alexander's time. In the temple stood 365 idols, one sacred to every day of the year. And the priests of the Capitol watched over the purity of the idols and made sure the faithful performed sacrifice on each day of the year, according to their custom.

But when Mary and the child entered the precinct of the Capitol, all the idols tumbled face down onto the ground and shattered into thousands of pieces. This was to show the Egyptians that the idols were false gods and to fulfill what Isaiah had said: "The Lord shall come on a swift cloud, and he will enter Egypt, and the idols made by hands will tumble down before his presence."

Word of this wonder came to Affrodosius, the governor of the city, and he sent his army out to arrest the ones who had caused the trouble. But when he entered the temple, he saw the idols face down and shattered on the floor, and Mary holding the child Jesus in her arms. Affrodosius saluted the child and then fell to his knees. Then he arose and faced his people:

"The gods of Egypt lay scattered in pieces before you. If this child were not strong with the power of one greater than these gods, then they would not now be lying on their faces, broken and useless. Our gods acknowledge this child of God. We would be wise to do so also, for we remember with sorrow what happened to our forefathers when they disbelieved Moses, and how Pharaoh and the whole army were drowned in the sea because they would not accept the wonders."

And from that time onward, all the people of Sotinen believed in the Lord God through his child Jesus. And the family stayed in the vicinity for a fortnight.

One day Jesus went out into the street and followed some children who were playing. But the children ran on ahead of him and disappeared into a house. The child Jesus knocked at the door of the house, and a woman greeted him. Jesus asked the woman where the children had gone, but she said only that no children were inside the house. "Right you are," Jesus replied, "but tell me: what are those over there in the furnace?"

And the woman replied, "Three-year-old goats."

"Right you are again," Jesus said, and he called the goats to him. And then the children in the form of goats came out into the street and began to skip and dance around Jesus.

When the mothers of the children saw it, they fell down on their knees in fear and cried, "Lord Jesus, we have never doubted that you are the good shepherd. We trust you have come to heal us and not to do us any harm" (for the women were anxious about the changes in their children).

And Jesus said, "I will have mercy on you poor handmaids. I will restore your children to you." And so he did, and he said, "Come children: let us play for a little while." And the goats were immediately changed back into children.

# XIII

# John and Jesus in Egypt

Now about this time, when Mary and Joseph and the child were still afraid to return to Bethlehem, Elizabeth was told by the man of light that she should join her kinswoman and the holy family in Egypt. There the boy would be safe from Herod, who still looked to kill him.

So Elizabeth took the child and wandered through the desert looking for Mary, but being very old she called John aside and said to him: "Son, I will not finish this journey with you. You must find Mary and the child on your own, for they will take you in." And with that, Elizabeth slumped down onto the sand and her spirit passed away.

Now John was seven years old when his mother died, and he sat weeping over her body, not knowing how she should be prepared for burial. In Jerusalem, the wicked king Herod died at the very hour that Elizabeth had told her death to John.

Far from the place where Elizabeth's body lay in the sand, the child Jesus sat playing at his mother's feet, while Mary wove a fine linen tunic for him. When he looked up at his mother, she saw that he had been crying, though he had not made a sound to suggest he was unhappy. And Mary said, "Son, why are you weeping? Has your father scolded you?"

But the Lord Jesus sees all and knows all, and so what had distressed him was a vision: there was the holy child John, lost in the desert, his mother's body beside him. And there was no one to comfort him.

"Mother," Jesus said, "I am crying because Elizabeth your cousin has died, and because my beloved John is weeping next to her body, with no one to turn to and no help for his grief." And when Mary heard this, she too began to weep. Jesus then consoled her: "Mother, be still: You will see your kinswoman again." And as he spoke a cloud of light came down and transported them, along with the woman Salome, to the very place where Elizabeth's body had fallen. And there in the wilderness of 'Ain Ka-rim was John sitting and weeping.

Jesus said to the cloud, "Leave us here in this place." And the cloud left them, but made such a noise that John fled from the body of his mother and started out into the desert. Jesus called out to him, "John—do not be afraid. I am Jesus your cousin and I have come with my virgin mother to see to your mother's burial, the blessed Elizabeth."

When the blessed John heard the voice calling him he turned back. And seeing Jesus and Mary standing there he ran to them. Mary embraced the child and Jesus held his hand, as children do. "Mother," said Jesus, "you and Salome must ready the body for burial. You must wash it."

Mary and Salome found a stream nearby, and with its water they prepared Elizabeth's body. And seeing the grief in the boy's face, the holy virgin Mary held John close and comforted him, and she cursed Herod for all the outrages he had committed against the children of Israel, for she did not know that God had taken Herod's spirit away at the moment of Elizabeth's death.

Then the angels Micha-el and Gabrhi-el came down from heaven to dig the grave. But Jesus said to them, "There are not enough here to mourn the death of the blessed woman Mart-Elizabeth. Go back and bring down with you the souls of Zechariah the priest, her husband who was killed by Herod, and the soul of the holy priest Simeon, who confessed me in the Temple. Let them sing while we bury the body." Micha-el did Jesus' bidding, and brought back with him the souls of Zechariah and Simeon. And the two priests shrouded the body and sang over it for a long while.

After seven days of mourning, Mary taught John the secrets of the desert: how he could clothe himself in camel-skin and eat locusts and wild honey to stay alive. But after John had been consoled and instructed, Jesus said to his mother, "We must leave him now to do his work, and I must go to do mine."

But Mary saw the loneliness on the holy John's face and she said to Jesus, "No. We cannot leave him here—he is a child of seven. We will take him with us and he will be like another son to your father and me."

But Jesus said:

> This is the will of my father in heaven:
> John will remain in the desert until the day
> he shows himself to Israel.
> He will walk among angels and prophets
> and not be touched by the wild beasts,
> and Gabrhi-el will be beside him
> with the sword of heaven to protect him.
> And the stream flowing here I will make
> as sweet as his mother's milk.
> Who has care for this boy, more than I?
> I have loved him more than all the world.

And these are the words which the Lord Jesus spoke to his blessed mother, who still wept for John. "Forgive me," she said to the boy as they departed. "Forgive me for leaving you out in the desert—with no Elizabeth to comfort you and no Zechariah to protect you. The world weeps with you today."

But Jesus said again, as the cloud of light appeared to whisk them away: "Mother, I say again: don't weep for John. He is truly blessed and I will not forget him." And the cloud lifted them out of the desert.[1]

# XIV

## The Child Jesus in Nazareth[1]

Mary, Joseph, and the child Jesus were in Egypt until word was received of the death of Herod the king. An angel appeared in a dream to Joseph and said, "Get up, and take the child and his mother and go home." And Joseph obeyed the angel, but discovered that Archelaus—a worse man than his father—had become king in Herod's place. And so Joseph set his mind on Nazareth in Galilee and led the family there. And there Jesus grew strong in mind and spirit, and he was about five years old when they came out of Egypt.

Jesus was always with Mary. She would take his hand and lead him along the roads, but he loved to be picked up, until his tired mother would say, "Sweet son, can't you walk just a little of the way?" And he would laugh and walk along beside her, untroubled. He hung on to her skirts with his little fingers—the one on whom the universe itself hangs—and looked up into her holy face. Then she would scoop him up again into her arms and walk a little further.

And one sabbath, while he was playing, the child Jesus wandered to a stream to play in the mud. And from the mud in his hands he crafted twelve little sparrows. And a certain teacher of the law, when he saw what Jesus was doing on the holy day, ran off to tell his father, Joseph. "Look," said the teacher, "I am not one to complain, but your son mocks the sabbath and needs to be set right."

Joseph looked up from his work and said, "How can this be so?"

"I have seen him at the stream fashioning pigeons out of the mud, and our law forbids this on the holy day."

So Joseph went along to the stream, and there he saw the child Jesus playing and the clay sparrows just beside him. Joseph was angry when he saw that the teacher had been right, and he shouted, "Why are you doing these things on the sabbath. You know this sort of thing is forbidden."

And when Jesus saw his father's anger he clapped his hands and the sparrows chirped and flew away into the sky. The children playing nearby and the teacher were astonished at this, and rumor soon spread that this child was no ordinary son of Israel.

Now when the son of Annas the scribe saw what Jesus could do, he took a branch from the willow tree and razed the mudpile where Jesus was playing and stomped through the puddles that Jesus had been using to wet his clay. And the child Jesus was very angry and said to the boy, "Why have you done this? What harm have I done to you? You'll pay for this foolishness." And as soon as he had said this, the son of Annas the scribe fell down, dead.

Annas the scribe and his wife came running when they heard that their son had been stricken by the word of the child Jesus.

And they picked up the body of their son and took it to Joseph, wailing along the road that the boy was too young to die. "Look," they said when they arrived at Joseph's door, "Look what your son has done. How can you abide a child that does this sort of thing?"

At this moment Jesus was coming home and heading through the village when another boy, a friend of the first, ran to Jesus and pushed him to the ground. And again, Jesus was angry, and he said,

"You'll run no further." And suddenly the boy fell to the ground, dead. Many people of Nazareth saw these things happen, and they wondered to themselves what could be done with a child who could slay with only a word.

And so the parents of the dead boy, and other villagers, came to the house of Joseph and said, "You must leave the village, or keep him indoors until he can learn to hold his tongue from cursing our children. For he seems to be able to kill with only a word."

Joseph called Jesus to him and scolded him: "My child, the people of this town hate us and will stone us if you persist in these deeds. Have you no thought for what will happen to your mother and father?"

And Jesus said, "You think as men think. But for your sake I will hold my peace. Only my accusers will be punished." And with this said, those who had complained to Joseph were struck blind. The people who witnessed this grumbled to themselves that Joseph could not keep the boy in check, but that he was something wild and unstoppable.

And Joseph was grieved when he heard this and decided to make an example of his discipline, so he took the child Jesus by the ear and pinched it and said, "Have you no regard at all for your father!"

But Jesus looked at him with lightning in his eyes and said, "My father? Who is my father? You are like them; you do not understand what is standing before you: Do not put me to the test."[2]

# XV

## Jesus and the Teachers

A certain teacher named Zakaius heard some of what Jesus had said to Joseph, and he was awed by the boy's eloquence and wisdom. So after a week he knocked at Joseph's door and he said, "I know that your child is very wise, but he is impudent and he lacks discipline. I can help you. Give him to me for lessons and I will teach him his letters. It's through letters, after all, that we learn respect for what our elders have to teach us. I will teach him to love his own and not to curse his elders, and to honor the tradition of the fathers throughout his life."

Joseph quickly agreed to Zakaius's plan and handed Jesus over to him for instruction. And Zakaius began by teaching the boy the alphabet from alpha to omega, and asked the boy to repeat the letters back to him again and again.

Jesus obliged Zakaius for a while, but then turned to him and said, "What is the meaning of the alpha?" But Zakaius did not understand and could not answer, and so Jesus asked again, "What is the true meaning of the alpha?"

Zakaius was silent.

Then Jesus said, "If you, a teacher, don't know the meaning of the alpha, then why do you move to beta and gamma?

By this time Zakaius's tongue was dry and he could not get the words out of his mouth. So Jesus said to him, "Listen, oh teacher of Israel, and I will explain to you the meaning of the letters." And within the hearing of the people Jesus went on to explain the letters from alpha to omega, with all of their secrets.

When Zakaius the teacher saw that the child knew more than he did, he said within earshot of all the people, " I am ashamed of myself for thinking that I could teach this lad anything. Please, Joseph, take him away. I can't bear the look in his eye when he judges my mistakes. I tell you this for certain: this little child is not earthly born. Why, even the fire would obey him. He seems to know everything since the beginning of the world. Joseph: What woman bore him? I have never seen anything like him—a boy who teaches the teacher and whose lessons, I confess, are very difficult for me to follow. And now let me go away in shame, because I have wronged you and deceived myself—first of all in thinking that I could make a disciple of the master, and second in letting myself think that my gray whiskers make me wise. But no, the wisdom of the world is in this young face. Let the rabbis taunt me as they will: I, Zakaius the teacher, have been bested in a contest with a child. I beg of you, Joseph, leave me in peace and comfortable in my ignorance and take the child—or is he a god or an angel?—back home with you."

And many of the rabbis tried to console the old teacher, who had fainted dead away from the strain but the child Jesus laughed and said,

> Those who are barren bear fruit
> Those who are blind in heart see;

And I have come from above
in order to confound the wisdom of the wise;
in order to impart the knowledge of things heavenly,
as I am commanded to do by Him who is above me.

When Jesus had finished speaking, all those who had disbelieved in him and had fallen under the curse were healed, and from that day on the people wondered about him and were hesitant to provoke him.

# XVI

## Jesus and the Child Zeno

A few days later, the child Jesus was playing in the upper room of a house, and one of his playmates, whose name was Zeno, lost his balance while climbing on the roof and fell down from the housetop and died. Jesus' playmates were afraid of being blamed for the accident and ran away terrified when they saw what had happened. But the child Jesus sat next to the dead boy until his parents came and saw what had happened.

And the boy's father said to Jesus, "You are responsible for this!" and began to scold him, though Jesus said to them again and again, "I have done nothing to hurt the boy."

And then Jesus stood up and commanded the child to rise and tell his parents how he had died, and immediately the child stood on his feet and said, "No, Lord, you did not throw me down: you raised me up." And from that instant the parents of the boy who had been dead worshiped Jesus as the Lord.[1]

# XVII

## Jesus Saves a Woodsman

After a time a young man of Nazareth was chopping wood, and was using his foot to steady the wood while he chopped. The man lost his balance and cleft his foot with the axe, and fell to the ground, ready to die from loss of so much blood. A crowd gathered around the young man, but there was nothing anyone could do. Some suggested calling a physician, but others said, "No, he is at the point of death; may as well wait to bury him."

Seeing the crowd, the child Jesus ran to find out what the noise was about, and he asked one of the bystanders what everyone was looking at. "This man has chopped his foot with an axe and is about to die," the boy was told. But Jesus made his way through the people and took hold of the young man's foot and said to him, "Get up: finish chopping your wood." And in the sight of everyone the man's foot was healed, and Jesus said to him, "Remember me."

The man fell down before Jesus and said, "Lord, I worship you," and when the crowd saw the sign they also said, "Lord, we worship you. The spirit of God truly dwells in this boy."

# XVIII

## The Miracle at the Well

There are many other things which the child Jesus did while he was with his parents in Nazareth. When he was six years old, his mother sent him to fetch some water in a jar. But on his way to the well, the child tripped and the pitcher was broken. So Jesus took his cloak and filled it with water, and the cloak held the water as though it were made of clay. And when Mary saw this she kissed the boy and kept to herself the mystery that was unfolding under her roof.

On another occasion[1] there was a wedding feast not far from Nazareth in the village of Cana in Galilee, and Mary took Jesus along with her while Joseph remained in Nazareth. In the middle of the feast, however, the wine ran out and the bridegroom was humiliated. So Mary came to Jesus and she said, "Son, the host has no more wine. You could help him if you wanted to." But Jesus looked at her and said, "You must not tell me what to do: I am not yet old enough to reveal myself."

But Mary knew that the child would be obedient, and so she said to the servants, "Do whatever he tells you to do."

And so Jesus pointed to the stone jars used for storing water: there were six of these, each holding about thirty gallons. And he said to the servants, "Fill these jars with water," and the servants did as they were instructed and filled the jars to the top. "Now," said Jesus, "take a ladle and draw some water from the top, and take it to the host." And again, the servants did what they were told, and took a bit of the water for the host to taste.

When the man in charge of the feast tasted the water he marveled and said, "Why, this isn't water at all. It is wine, and not only that: it is the best wine of the day. Most people serve the best wine first and save the bad for later, when people have drunk too much to notice, but the bridegroom has kept the best wine for last!" And Jesus and his mother and brothers stayed on a while in Cana.[2]

# XIX

## Jesus and His Father

There are many things which caused Joseph to marvel as well. One day when Jesus was eight years old, he joined his father in the fields to sow wheat, for the time for sowing had arrived. And as Joseph toiled in the field, Jesus sowed one kernel of wheat and instantly it grew and he threshed it and it made a hundred measures of wheat.[1] So he called the poor of the village to the threshing floor and gave them the wheat and gave Joseph what was left over.

Since Joseph was a carpenter, he made his living from crafting yokes and ploughs. But from time to time he would make other things as well. One day an order arrived from a very rich man of Nazareth who wanted a bed made for him. But in making the bed, Joseph noticed that one beam was too short and did not know what to do about it; so the young child Jesus said to him, "Father, lay down two pieces of wood and make them even against your chest," and Joseph did as the child told him.

Jesus stood at the other end and took hold of the shifting beam, which was the shorter one, and stretched it, making it equal to the other. His father Joseph saw it and was amazed, and he kissed the child and praised God, saying, "Lord, I thank you for the gift of this boy."

But after a time Joseph began to worry, and thought again that it was time for Jesus to learn his letters. So he searched about for another teacher for Jesus, one who would be able to handle the child better than Zakaius had managed to do. And when a teacher had been found, he said to Joseph, "I will deal with the boy; I have heard all about him and what he did to the old teacher Zakaius. But I have other methods. I will teach him the Greek letters and then the Hebrew." So Joseph left the child in the care of the teacher.

First the teacher wrote down the letters in Greek and Jesus pondered over them for a long time. Then he said to the teacher, "If you are the teacher, tell me the meaning of the alpha, and then I will tell you the power of the beta." But the teacher lost patience and wrung Jesus' ear in anger. Jesus cried out in pain and then called down God's wrath on the teacher, and instantly the teacher fell dead to the ground.

The child went home to Joseph and told him what had taken place and how the teacher had hurt him. But Joseph was at a loss and could not decide what to do, so he said to Mary: "Keep him inside the house, for those who provoke him are subject to God's wrath."

But Joseph, after a while, decided to turn the child over for instruction to yet another teacher—a faithful friend of his—who assured him that he was not afraid of the child's wisdom. Joseph agreed, saying, "If indeed you are not afraid of him, then by all means see if he will bend to your instruction."

And the teacher came to Joseph's door, acting very brave, though within his heart he was troubled and afraid. Jesus followed the teacher happily to school. Once inside, the teacher gave Jesus a book from the shelf and asked him, "Child, can you read the letters written here?" And Jesus took the book from the teacher and began to read—not the letters in the book, but the letters of the holy spirit.[2] And he began to teach the people assembled in the place the whole law of Moses, and many people who were passing by the door of the school stopped to listen and to marvel at the wisdom given to a child. "Is this Joseph's son," they wondered; "is this the son of Mary, the brother of James?"

When Joseph got word that Jesus was once again the subject of rumor, he ran off to the school thinking that this teacher, too, was in for trouble. But when he arrived at the door, he saw the crowd standing around and marveling at every word that came out of the child's mouth. And he saw the teacher too, standing in the place usually taken by the pupil while Jesus taught him along with the others. The teacher said to Joseph, "My friend, I took this child on as a pupil thinking that I could teach him something, but this boy is full of grace and wisdom from the spirit of God himself. There is nothing he needs to learn: take him home."

And Jesus smiled and said, "Teacher, you deserve credit for speaking the truth about me. And for your sake, your brothers will also be healed." And at that instant the other teacher rose from the ground and was healed. And Joseph took Jesus home to supper.

# XX

## Jesus and James

Now one day Joseph sent his son James to gather some sticks for fuel and Jesus skipped along behind him, for he loved James especially. And as James was binding the sticks with a cord, a viper bit him on the hand.

Jesus had been playing at a distance when this happened, and when he found James his hand was swollen and he was at the point of death. But Jesus breathed on the hand and the poison leaked away, and the arm became whole again.

Jesus then spotted the serpent as it slithered away toward the brush, and he said to it, "For what you have done to my brother James, you will not finish your journey." And the serpent swelled up and burst.[1]

Around the same time, a child got sick and died, and his mother would not be comforted. Jesus heard of the mother's sorrow and ran to the house where she was bent over the body of the dead boy, weeping and wailing. And Jesus approached the bed and touched the child on the breast and said, "Child, do not be dead: live for your mother." And instantly the child sat up and looked at his mother and laughed. Jesus then looked at the mother and said, "Take the boy and nurse him. Remember me."

There were many witnesses to these things. and everyone who saw what the child was able to do was astonished. "Either he is a god or an angel of God," they said, "because everything he wants to do he is able to do." But Jesus had gone from the house and was in the street playing with the children.[2]

# XXI

# The Rich Man Ibram

There was a certain rich man in the city named Ibram, who was building a great house in order to impress the people of Nazareth. One day Ibram came to inspect the building and complained to the builders that the roof was too low to be seen outside the city. "I want my house to be seen from seven miles out," he said, and so the builders built it higher.

Ibram came again to inspect, but again he was disappointed, "Look," he said, "I do not pay you good money for you to build me a beggar's hovel. My roof must be seen from ten miles out." And so the builders went to work, making a high tower on the house that could be seen from far beyond the city. Ibram stationed a servant and his camel ten miles out in the desert.

Then he climbed to the top of his house and strained to see them, but he could not. But in straining to see where his servant had gone, he lost his balance and fell from the roof, dead, to the ground. The poor of the city gathered around him and mumbled, "It serves him right. He was trying to rival the very temple of God in beauty."

But Jesus came along and saw the dead man lying in the street and he said to the crowd, "He has learned his lesson. For the rich and the poor alike are subject to the judgment of God," and he took Ibram's hand and said to him, "Get up and go about your work. But remember who saved you and give the credit to God." And Ibram looked at the child and said, "This boy is from heaven: he saves men from death and pities even the rich."

# XXII

# Jesus and the Doctors of the Law

When he was twelve years old[1] the parents of Jesus went up to Jerusalem according to their custom for the feast of Passover. Afterward, they were on their way back to Nazareth, supposing that Jesus was playing farther back in the caravan, when they discovered he had returned to Jerusalem on his own. They searched the city for three days, asking friends and kinfolk whether anyone had heard from the child, but at every stop they were disappointed.

Joseph, however, decided to consult the priests to find out what he might do to recover his lost son and finally made his way to the temple precincts. When he entered he saw something marvelous, for there in the midst of the wisest men of Israel was the child Jesus, who was teaching the law of Moses to the sages. They sat at attention while Jesus asked them questions and silenced the elders and teachers when they tried to dispute any point with him. Nothing like this had been seen in Israel before.

Mary approached him and said, "Son: you have been a great

112

worry to your father and me. We have looked for you all over the city, and thought you were lost to us forever."

Jesus said to Mary, "Why have you been looking for me along the way and in the city, when you might have known that I would be about my father's business here."

And a scribe said to Mary, "Are you the mother of this child?"

Mary answered, "I am."

And the scribe said,

Blest are you among women Mary,
>     for the fruit of your womb is holy.
>     From now on, all generations shall bless you
>     as God has richly blessed you.
>     For this child has put down the mighty from their chairs
>     and scattered the proud in their heart's conceit.
>     he has kept the promise made to our ancestors,
>     and has come to teach his servant Israel.
>     he has shown mercy to Abraham's children.[2]

And the teachers of the law said that they had never seen wisdom or eloquence like the child's in Israel.

But Jesus arose and followed Mary and was obedient to Joseph, while Mary kept secret in her heart the angel's assurance that the child was the messiah, the word of God himself. And returning to Nazareth, Jesus grew even stronger in wisdom.

# XXIII

## The Silly Teacher

Jesus walked along beside his mother on the way to the market and along the way they saw a teacher giving a lesson to some pupils.

Now just above the teacher's head on a wall some sparrows were chirping noisily and quarreling over scraps of bread, when suddenly all twelve of the sparrows fell from the wall into the teacher's lap. The pupils laughed, and Jesus stopped dead in his tracks at the commotion, and then he laughed too, seeing the frustration on the teacher's face.[1]

But the teacher did not think things so funny, so he said to one of his pupils, "See that boy over there? Go and bring him to me."

The boy did so, and the teacher, as soon as he could reach it, took hold of Jesus' ear and began to wring it till it was sore: Then he said, "Boy: what were you laughing about just now?"

And Jesus said, "I laughed because I caused the birds to drop into your lap."

The teacher was puzzled and said to Jesus, "How so? Were you the cause of their squawking?"

And Jesus said, "Yes: the bread they fought over was my gift to them, and the squawking was to interrupt your lesson since you have nothing worth teaching these children."[2]

The teacher was humiliated in front of his students, but did not try to correct Jesus, for news of the child's powers had spread very widely. So Jesus said to the teacher, "Pray for grace from God, and pray to find understanding." And Jesus went along to the market-place with his mother, singing sweetly as he skipped beside her.

# XXIV

# The Miracle of the Dyer

One day Mary visited a neighbor of hers who made her living dying wool. Jesus went along beside his mother, singing happily as he always did when he was near her. And while Mary struck up a conversation with her neighbor at the doorpost, Jesus wandered into the dyer's house and found the tables inside spread with pots and jars. Some of the jars were empty; others contained the dyes used by the dyer in her craft. Piled next to the pots on the table were cloths and bolts of yarn, which people had brought to the woman's house for dying.

Jesus gathered all of the cloth and all of the yarn into a bundle; then he sunk the lot in a large pot which contained only black dye. Just as he had done this the dyer came into the house to see what Jesus was up to, and when she saw what had happened she was vexed and wailed to Jesus' mother: "Mary," she said, "look what the boy has done! I have spent days making the dyes and sorting the cloths, and now just look: all of my work has come to nothing."

And Mary said to Jesus, "Child, this is a very bad thing. You

116

have ruined a week's work, and there is no way we can repay the damage you have done."

Jesus said to Mary, "I am not sure what you mean. You say I have destroyed her work—and that there is no way to repair the damage?"

Mary grew impatient when she heard Jesus speak this way, and she said, "Child: I have always loved you, and you have always been the apple of my eye. But today you are a thorn in your mother's heart. Why do you taunt me?"

Jesus said again, "Mother, you say I have destroyed this good woman's work. How have I done so?"

"See here," said Mary, "a dyer uses many colors for her work, and each of the cloths was meant to be a different color. You have sunk all of the cloths into one pot, and they are now all black." And Mary implored the woman to forgive her.

But Jesus, when he saw this, smiled and walked over to the pot where he had sunk the cloths into black dye, and he put in his hand. One by one he pulled out the cloths and the bolts of wool, each one being the color it was meant to be dyed: purple, red, white, and crimson—each one perfectly done, without any mixture of colors and without any imperfections.

When the dyer saw what Jesus had done, she fell to her knees and said to the child: "Who are you? How can I repay you for what you have done? Not only is my lot not ruined, but you have made my work light by making every cloth its proper color."

But Jesus said only, "You have my mother to thank. I have done this for her sake." And Mary took the child in her arms and kissed him. Then she returned with the boy to the house of Joseph.

# XXV[1]

## The Children in the Oven

Not many days later, Jesus went out to play with some children, but being frightened of his powers they ran away from him and took refuge in a potter's oven. Not long thereafter, the potter came along and, not knowing the boys were inside, put some new pots into the oven for firing, stoked the fire, and waited for his work to be done.

The mother of one of the children saw Jesus standing nearby, and she said to him, "Child, have you seen my son?"

And Jesus said, "Yes. But I see him no longer."

Soon, the mother of another of the boys came to where Jesus was standing, near to the potter's oven, and she said, "Child, my son was playing in the vicinity. Have you seen him playing?"

And Jesus answered, "Yes, but he plays no longer."

A third mother then came along, and she said to Jesus, "We know your reputation. What have you done with our sons?"

And Jesus said, "I have done nothing. When I came to play, they avoided me and ran into the oven."

When the women heard this they wept and tore at their garments. "He has destroyed our sons!"

But Jesus said, "Your sons are not dead: they live. Sheep, come out and find your shepherd." And when he opened the door of the furnace, out came three young lambs who skipped merrily around Jesus and then went over to the women.

When the women saw this they were afraid: "Jesus, son of Mary," they said, "we know you have come to heal and not to destroy. You are the shepherd of Israel: have mercy on us women."

Jesus saw that the women did not understand the sign that had been given to them, so he said, "The children of Israel are like these sheep: they cannot tell their true shepherd. Instead, they follow the inclinations of their hearts."

But the women said, "Child, son of Mary, we know that you are the true shepherd of these children and that they are ours only by birth. Restore them to their former state and they will be your followers: they will not harass their true shepherd; they will never hide themselves from you again—because we know that it is impossible to hide anything from God."[2]

When Jesus heard the women's plea he said to them, "Daughters of Israel: you speak wisely. These children will be my followers." And straightaway the sheep were changed back to children. Then Jesus said, "Come, little children, and be my playmates."

And they laughed and happily followed after Jesus, and did not desert him from that day on. And their mothers admonished them strictly, "Make sure that you do everything that Jesus, the son of Mary, asks of you."

# XXVI

## The Funeral of Joses

Joseph received word that a son of his had died in Capernaum, and he took Jesus with him to join in the mourning. On the day of the gathering, Jesus saw his father crying and said to him, "Father, what is all this weeping about?"

Joseph hushed him and said, "Boy, my firstborn, Joses, is to be buried today and it is our custom to weep for the dead."

But Jesus looked at his father quizzically and said, "These men do not know why they are weeping. If they did, they would not weep for the dead but for themselves."

Again Joseph hushed the boy, but Jesus said, "Father, take the shawl that covers your head and lay it on Joses' face."

Joseph was hesitant, but he knew that Jesus was filled with the spirit of God, and so he laid his headcovering on the face of Joses. But nothing happened. Joseph was vexed and said to Jesus, "Now I am scandalized in front of my brothers. It is not our custom to touch the dead!"

But Jesus smiled and said, "Father, he is not dead. Take your headcovering and go, touch Joses' face and say, 'God saves us.' "

Joseph was even more hesitant, but he did as Jesus told him to do and laid his headcovering on Joses' face saying, "God saves us."

Instantly Joses rose from the bier and asked, "Why is everyone hereabouts weeping and wailing? Has someone died?"

And the mourners were astonished and fled from Jesus. But Joses approached the boy and said, "Child, who has done this? For I know I was very sick, and must have died, and this funeral is nobody else's but my own."

And Jesus said, "My father in heaven has done this. The power of his Christ has done this. For he is a God of the living and not of the dead."

# XXVII

# The Interim

When Jesus returned with Joseph from the funeral at Capernaum, and everyone in the house had heard of his wonders, Joseph threw a feast in honor of Jesus' birthday. And Joseph's children James, Joseph, Juda, and Simeon were there, along with Mary and Jesus and the other Mary.[1] When Jesus came into the room he blessed them and gathered them around the table.

No one dared to eat or drink before he did, and always after this time his mother and Joseph, and the sons and daughters of Joseph showed him deference and protected him. And when he slept, the radiance of God shone above his bed. To God be praise and glory for ever, amen!

# XXVIII

## The Baptism

John, the son of Elizabeth, had come out of the desert of Egypt and into Judaea where he baptized and preached. And he was dressed as Mary had instructed him: in camel hair, with a leathern belt; and he had survived since childhood on locusts and wild honey.[1]

This was the same John foretold by Isaiah when he said, "Someone is shouting in the desert, 'Prepare a road for the Lord; make the road easier for him to travel.' "

People came from the surrounding area, from Jerusalem and Judaea and villages along the Jordan, and they begged to be baptized by the young John. But when some Pharisees and Sadducees came to him to be washed, he said to them, "You vipers: and who told you that washing would help you to escape the punishment of God? Do what is necessary to show that you have put aside your wickedness. It is impossible to escape by saying 'We have Abraham as our father,' because God can make children of Abraham from the rocks. Listen: the axe is being swung at the roots of the trees, and every tree that looks dead will be cut down and heaped on the fire. What

I am doing is washing with water, washing those who have repented: the one who is coming will baptize you with the spirit of God—and with the fire. He is greater than I am. I am not worthy to fasten his sandals; and this one comes with his sickle to thresh the grain. The one I speak of will gather the wheat into the barn, but he will burn the chaff in an unquenchable fire."

So John spoke, and the people came. And around this time[2] Jesus came up from his father's house in Nazareth to be baptized by John, and when John saw him he said, "I ought to be baptized by you: why do you come to me?"

Jesus looked at John and said, "Let God's purposes be fulfilled in this way; we must do what God asks." And John agreed, and he washed Jesus.

And as soon as Jesus had emerged from the water, heaven opened and he saw the spirit of God coming down like a dove and lighting on him; and a voice from heaven said, *This is my beloved child in whom I delight.*[3]

But the spirit of God drove Jesus into the desert, where he remained for forty days and forty nights without food. Jesus was very hungry and the Tempter came to him and said, "You are God's son, I hear, the child of no earthborn father. If that is so, why not make these stones bread?"

Jesus said to the Tempter, "Because scripture says 'Man cannot live on bread alone; he needs the words of God.' "[4]

And the Tempter took Jesus to the holy city of Jerusalem, and sat him down on the pinnacle of the Temple there and said to him, "You are the son of God, I hear, and not of any earthborn father: If that is so, why not hurl yourself down. For scripture says, *'God will order his angels to hold you up in their arms so that your feet will not be hurt upon the stones.'* "[5]

Jesus answered the Tempter saying, "Scripture says as well, *'Do not test the Lord your God.'* "

Then Jesus was taken to a very high mountain, where the Tempter showed him all the kingdoms of the world and he said, "I can make you prince over all of these; all you must do is fall down on your knees and worship me."

But Jesus said, "Away with you, Satan: scripture says 'Worship the Lord your God, him only shall you worship.' "[6]

And instantly the Tempter left him and he was alone in the desert, except for the wild beasts who flocked around him and worshiped him and the angels who ministered to him.

On his return to Judaea, Jesus was walking alone and was very hungry[7] from his time in the desert. In the distance he saw a fig tree covered with leaves, so he went to see whether there were any figs on the tree. But when he came closer, he saw that there were only leaves, since the season was not right for figs. And Jesus said to the tree: "You are cursed because you have not borne fruit when I was hungry," and there were some standing around who heard him say this.

The next morning as Jesus walked along the road, he saw that the fig tree had withered and died, all the way down to the roots. One of the bystanders remembered what he had said the day before, that the tree was cursed because it had not borne fruit when Jesus was hungry, and he said, "How is this possible: yesterday the tree was covered with leaves, today it is dead to the roots." Jesus looked at him and said, "With God all things are possible."

It was about this time that Jesus received news of the death of John, whom he loved more than all others. And going to the place where John had been buried, Jesus entered the tomb, and he touched the body where it lay, and said, "John, arise!" And John rose up and looked at Jesus and loved him.[8]

# XXIX

## The Death of Joseph

Now the time came for Jesus to leave the house of Joseph for good. His mother had kept everything close to her heart, but when he was ready to depart she called him aside and said,[1]

> Grace and truth are joined
> > Righteousness and peace kiss each other
> > Truth flourishes out of the earth
> > and Righteousness looks on you from heaven.

"All of the prophets have spoken of you, from David onward. When you were little, before the spirit came on you,[2] you were out one day with Joseph in the fields. All of a sudden there was a rush of wind, and through the door walked your very likeness—which I thought was you. But the likeness said to me, 'Where is Jesus, my brother? I want to play with him.' "

"And I thought you were teasing me. But the likeness—which was really the spirit of the power of God—looked at me until I became confused and thought it was a spirit come to tempt me. So I took the likeness and I tied it to the bedpost and rushed out in the fields to where you were working with your father.

"And I told everything to Joseph, who would not believe me and wanted to see for himself. But as I looked at you, I knew that you had already understood the affair, and you laughed and said, 'Where is this likeness, so that I can see it?' And Joseph went with us into the house and found the likeness bound to the bed—and we looked at it, and then at you and realized that you were his perfect image; so we loosened the knot and freed the spirit, and it ran to you, embraced you and you him, and the two became one."

From that time, Jesus went about Nazareth healing and casting out spirits from those who were possessed. It was during this time that Jesus, the son of God, was called upon to comfort his mother, for Joseph was very old. His sons Joses and Simeon had married and only James remained at home to look after his father's business. Joseph called his children to him, and Mary and Jesus, and he said, "I know that I will die very soon. I must make one last journey to the Temple in Jerusalem to ask forgiveness of my sins."

Mary objected, thinking that so hard a journey would hasten the death of her husband, but Jesus said, "Let him be: for he is a righteous man and craves to be with God when he dies."

And so, Jesus, Mary, and Joseph went once again to Jerusalem and Joseph prayed in the Temple:

> It was you who brought me
>     safely through birth
>     and when I was young you
>     kept me safe.
> I have done what you require
>     since the day I was born,
>     I have depended on you,

127

> O God my strength.
> But now trouble is near:
> I am old and afflicted in body;
> Do not be far away from me.

Joseph prayed to God at the altar to die a peaceful death and to enter into the glory of God. And on the way back to Nazareth, his strength at last gave way and entering the house, Mary and Jesus helped him onto his bed. Joseph called to Jesus to be near him, and he said to him:

"My child, I have loved you as my own, but I have known from the first that you belong really to God. This I was told by an angel of light, sent from God to strengthen me when I was ready to divorce your holy mother. And now I pray that God will forgive me for my doubt. You are God's son, but even so I have protected you. Do you remember, when you were still very small, how the blame was laid on you for the death of a boy who'd been bitten by a viper? When his family discovered him, they were ready to take you to Herod, and knowing your power, I also blamed you in the matter. But then, you took the boy's arm and commanded him to rise, and he did. His parents rejoiced at this, I recall, but I was less happy at these displays. So I took you by the ear and I said to you, 'Hush! Hide the light of your power, lest you bring down the wrath of neighbors on your father's house.'

"But you looked at me and said, 'Beloved father: I call you father even though my father is above, you still do not understand the angel's message. I do what my true father asks of me; if you understood that, you would not wring my ear or be angry.' "

When he had said this, Joseph closed his eyes and Mary said to Jesus, "Must Joseph die?" Jesus said, "Yes, mother; all must die, but Joseph will enter into the glory of God because he has been a father to me and has protected me."

With this said, Jesus sat at the head of Joseph's bed, and Mary at the foot, and Jesus felt the old man's throat with his holy hand and said, "The time has come: his soul is in his throat."³

And Mary felt his legs—cold as ice—and they had gone very stiff; so Joseph's brothers and sisters, and his children were called to mourn at his passing. And the first to enter the house was his daughter Lysia, a trader in purple, who wept when she saw her father. The other children came as well, and all wept and clutched their shirts, for they loved Joseph very much.

Jesus then glanced at the door, and saw Death⁴ with all of his gruesome attendants: there was Amente, and there were the demons armed with fire; but Jesus rebuked all of them that had claims on Joseph's soul, and he told Death to wait until he was permitted to enter the room. So Death waited beyond the door, and Amente and the demons and attendants armed with fire fled at Jesus' command. Then Jesus prayed to his Father:

> Father,
> your will be done;
> take the soul of your servant,
> the holy Joseph,
> safely through the heavens;
> protect him from the princes of darkness
> who rule the air,
> for his faith has not weakened;
> like Abraham, when he thought
> of his body, or of his possessions,
> his faith did not bend:
> His faith did not leave him, because
> he remained true to God's promises,
> and he never doubted.
> His faith filled him with power,

and he was confident that God
would do what he had promised.
Now, let the river of fire be to him
like warm water; and let
the demons be far away from vexing him.

And Jesus and all of Joseph's children said, *"Amen"* to this. And Mary's face took on a radiant appearance, as though she had been changed into an angel of light. Just then, it was as though the roof of the house split asunder and the angels of heaven came rushing down: Micha-el, Gabrhi-el, who had first given the message to Joseph, and a choir of others. But Death, seeing this, was afraid to enter the house, and so Jesus went out to him and said, "Abbaton: come in and do what you have to do. Only be gentle with this man, for he has been the spouse of my holy mother and protected the son of the living God."

Abbaton went into the house at sunrise, and he took the soul of Joseph from his lips and tried to steal away to the Kingdom of Darkness. But Gabrhi-el and Micha-el caught Death by the heel and took back the soul of Joseph. For safekeeping, they placed the soul in a silk purse and carried it on high to God, singing:

God sits on his sacred throne
he rules over the nations
More powerful than armies is he;
he rules supreme.[5]

Jesus went to the bed of Joseph and touched his eyes and closed his mouth; he consoled his mother and the children of Joseph; then, all the people of Nazareth came to mourn until the ninth hour, when Jesus himself anointed and washed the body, and he blessed it and prayed over it with prayers inscribed by the power of the spirit on the tablets of heaven before he became flesh. Then, a host of angels came down and shrouded the body.

## The Death of Joseph

When all of this had been done, the body was given to the chief men of Nazareth for burial, and when they entered the house they found Jesus weeping as he prayed:

> I call to you, Lord; help me now!
> Listen to me when I call to you.
> Receive my prayer like incense,
> my uplifted hands as an evening sacrifice.
> Like wood that is split
> and made into bits,
> so are the bones of the dead
> scattered at the edge of the grave.[6]

# XXX

# The Sleep and Awakening of Mary, Virgin and Mother[1]

[A]fter the death of Jesus] it was Mary's custom to go to the place where he had been laid to burn incense. And there she would implore the one who had been born of her that she could be taken away from this earth and joined with him again.

The priests had been spying on her, and noticed that she came to the sepulcher again and again, so they complained to the chief priest, and he ordered a guard to be posted outside the tomb with these instructions: "Let no one go near the tomb to pray."

And thus they were posted. Again and again Mary went to the tomb, and the guards did not see her,[2] but the evidence of her habits continued to accumulate and finally the priests complained to the high priest about the guard. Finally, the high priest called the guards to account: "I thought you were told to let no one near the tomb." The guards insisted that they had not been neglectful of their duty. Neither the priests nor the guards knew that God had prevented them from seeing her devotions.

On a Friday, holy Mary came to the tomb and prayed and

burned incense, when all of a sudden the heavens opened and the angel Gabrhi-el came to her and said:

> Praise to you,
>> bearer of Christ our God.
>> We have heard your prayer and Christ grants you
>> the privilege of joining him forever
>> in the heavenly places.

Now at this time, Mary was living in Bethlehem[3] with women disciples who were always at her side. When she returned home, she prayed, "Lord Jesus Christ, I beg you to send John to me, as you promised, and your other followers as well, so that I may see them and speak with them. Send me those who are far and those near, those who are awake and those who have died before me. I know that you will hear my prayer and grant my request."[4]

John came almost at once to her door, though he had been preaching the Word in Ephesus and was transported to Bethlehem on a cloud. And entering the house, John saw Mary lying down on her bed, and he said, "Mother of my Lord, you should be happy because you are leaving this world in great glory."

But Mary said, "I hope it may be true, but I am under indictment by the priests for worshiping at the tomb of my son, our Lord; and they have sworn that if I am discovered they will burn my body."

But John said, "Our Lord has promised you that your body will not see corruption." And at that, a rush of wind was heard and a voice from above said, *"Amen."* John listened to the voice and knew it to be the voice of the Holy Spirit, and he stood to pray: "Our Lord, Jesus Christ, comes, and you will behold him again, just as he promised you."

Then John heard the Holy Spirit[5] saying to all of the apostles: "Gather together wherever you are: Peter at Rome, Paul from

Tiberias, Thomas from India, James in Jerusalem, Andrew and Philip and Luke and Simon the Canaanite, and Thaddeus, who are dead—rise up from your sepulchers; but do not think the resurrection has come; you are being raised up by the Spirit from your graves to pay homage to the mother of your savior, Jesus Christ, for the day of her going to heaven is here."[6]

So all of the apostles were gathered together in the house of Mary,[7] having been transported from the ends of the earth on clouds of glory. And Mark, who was still alive, came from Alexandria in order to pay homage to the mother of his redeemer.

All of them gathered together in the house of Mary, and each one spoke of how he had been marvelously caught up in the air and transported to Bethlehem: some had been preaching, some baptizing, some on the road between towns when the cloud of light appeared, and each apostle in turn told the mother of God how they had come to be with her. When they had finished, Mary spread her hands and said, "LORD, glorify my name; let all generations call me blessed."

And instantly there was a peal of thunder and the room shook and the terrible sound of approaching chariots was heard. Seraphim surrounded the house with light. Then the sun and the moon swirled around the house in a yellow and white blaze and tombs fell open: the dead who had believed in Christ came out of their graves[8] and in the city, the lame got up and walked, the leprous were healed of their scabs, and those possessed were cleansed.

Word spread that anyone who so much as touched the wall of the house where the Virgin lived would be cleansed or healed, and many came to see things for themselves. People from all parts of Judaea began to gather outside her door and shout, "Holy Mary, Mother of God, pray for the sins of the world, have mercy on us," and all were healed.

But the priests grew more and more concerned, and decided that something must be done to put a stop to the goings-on in Bethlehem. And so they devised a plot against Mary and the apostles who were gathered there. An army was sent to burn down the house, and to destroy everyone in it; but along the way, the regiment was stopped dead in its tracks and fell down about a mile outside the city, as though their feet had been bound.

When word of this wonder got back to the priests, they were enraged and begged the governor to drive the woman away from Bethlehem, and all those who were with her in the house. But the governor wavered, because he believed that wonderful things were taking place in Bethlehem. Angrily the priests reminded him that, as an officer of the peace, he could be reported to Caesar if he did not put a stop to the mobs. And so the governor sent a contingent of one thousand men to arrest Mary and the apostles in Bethlehem.

But the Spirit spoke to Mary: "The governor is sending an army against you. Do not be afraid; leave the house." And Mary and the apostles did as they were told by the Spirit. And when they went outside, they found themselves not in Bethlehem but in Jerusalem, by the power of the Spirit, the protector.

When the soldiers reached Bethlehem, they found the house deserted, and took news of the wonder back to the governor. And no one in Bethlehem could explain the events to the soldiers, for no one had seen them leave the house.

After a few days, however, word spread that Mary had returned to her family's house in Jerusalem, and that the apostles stood by her to protect her. Multitudes of people who remembered the wonderful things done by Jesus stood around the house and prayed, "O holy virgin, mother of our redeemer, do not forget us when you come into his kingdom." But others in the city were enraged by the gathering, and they gathered wood to lay round the house, intending to burn it to the ground and to scorch everyone inside. The priests brought torches and the crowd marched toward the house of Mary, and the governor could do nothing to stop it.

When the crowd reached the house, one of the priests holding a torch aloft opened the door to fling it in and set the place ablaze; and instantly, a rush of flame swept over the crowd, breathed by an angel of God as a warning; and many in the crowd were burned badly in the flames. But all who had seen it glorified God and the Virgin who had given birth to the savior.

News of the affair spread rapidly, and came to the governor's ears. And when he had heard the story of the flames, he stood before the Jews and he said, "Now I, too, know that this Mary is the mother of God and the savior of the world was born of this virgin. These are the signs of a true God." But there was yet division among the Jews. Many believed because of the signs but many refused to believe in his name.

After all of these things happened, the Holy Spirit spoke to the apostles and said, "Remember Mary, the mother of God and virgin: it was on the Lord's day that the goods news of the birth of the savior was made known through the angel Gabrhi-el; and it was on the Lord's day that the savior was born in Bethlehem."[9]

And it was on the Lord's day that the children of Jerusalem sang hosanna to the highest son of David, blest is he who comes in the Lord's name; and it was on the Lord's day that he rose from the dead; and on the Lord's day he will come to judge the living and the dead. Know also that on the Lord's day the son will return for the glory and honor of his precious and holy mother.

Now it was the Lord's day when the Spirit said these things, and while he spoke, Mary was at prayer, when suddenly there was a rush of wind and the heavens broke open. Cherubim and seraphim descended on clouds, and behind them the glorious son of man, Christ Jesus the Lord. An incomparable light then shone on the face of his holy mother; it was the heavenly light, never before seen,[10] and it came from the son. When it shone, all the powers of heaven who dwell in the light fell down and worshiped.

And Jesus called to his mother and said, "Mary."

She said, "Here I am."

And Jesus said to her, "Do not be afraid. You have been given the power to behold the glory of God himself, the grace never before given to a mortal." And when Mary looked up, she saw glory which words have no power to describe. And Jesus said to her, "Today you will be translated into heaven, body and spirit; your soul will be a star in the heavens of the Father."

Mary said, "Son and Lord, lay your right hand upon me and bless me," and she looked, expecting to see in his wrists the mark of the spikes.

But the glorious Christ stretched out a pure and unblemished hand and laid hold of her, and she kissed it tenderly and said: "I worship this hand, the hand of my own dear son, and the hand which made heaven and earth. And I ask you to save my body and soul with your unstained right hand and take me with you into your kingdom forever. I ask you also to help the whole race of humankind, who call on you for salvation. Listen to them and answer their prayers, as you have often listened to me."

As Mary spoke, the apostles gathered around her feet and said, "Mother of our savior, do not leave us to destruction!"

And Mary prayed with hands uplifted:

> God, who in your great goodness
> sent your only begotten son
> to dwell in my poor body,
> who desired to be born of me,
> a lowly handmaiden of the Word,
> have mercy on the world—
> have mercy upon every soul
> who calls on your name.

And she prayed a second time:

O God, king of the heavens,
>Son of the living God,
>Accept everyone who calls on your name;
>and let your birth be glorified.
>O Lord Jesus;
>You have all power in heaven
>and on the earth.
>I call on your holy name
>to grant this prayer:
>At every time and every place
>where my name is invoked,
>make that place holy,
>and bless those that bless you
>through my name.
>Accept their prayers.

And when she had prayed, Jesus said to his mother, "My father in heaven has heard your petition, and you may know for certain that anyone who calls on your name will be heard, because every gift and grace has been given to you."

Then the Lord turned to Peter and said, "The time has come to prepare. Arise, Peter, take the body of Mary to the part of the city that I will show you, and in the east you will find a new sepulcher. There you shall put the body—and then wait for me to come to you."

Then Mary fell down, praising God and saying, "Lord, you have chosen to commit a sacred mystery to me. Receive my soul and do not let the prince of darkness have power over me."

Jesus said to her, "When I was sent by my father, the prince of darkness came to me and tried to tempt me; but he could find no sign of wickedness in me, and so he went away beaten. When you meet him, you will meet him as all mortals must—that is, according to death. But he will not conquer you, as he did Joseph, because I will be there to help you. So come with me to the joy of paradise."

Mary rose from the ground and laid herself on her bed, and praising God for the mystery, she gave up her soul. And the apostles saw her soul rise from her lips—a whiteness that words cannot describe, whiter than snow, more beautiful than silver, and glistening with the brightness of starlight.

And Jesus delivered the soul of Mary to Micha-el the angel, who ushered it to paradise. Gabrhi-el was there as well, and the Savior was taken back into heaven with the angels.

According to custom the women who were in Mary's house washed the body and anointed it to prepare it for burial. But when it was stripped of clothing, the body was so luminously bright that—although it could be touched—it could not be looked at, because the flashes of light were dazzling to the eye. Its splendor was so great that washing it added nothing to it: It was pure, beautiful and undefiled; it showed no mark of age, no sign of defilement or impurity. And from the body the scent of lilies arose, a sweetness that the senses cannot comprehend.

The apostles laid the body of Mary on a bier and wondered among themselves who should bear the palm ahead of it. John said to Peter, "You are the first among the apostles, and by rights you should carry the palm." But Peter shook his head. "No," he said, "You were the one chosen by the Lord to be her consolation, and you were very dear to our master: when he hung on the tree, he committed her to you with his own mouth: you take the palm before her bier and we will take the body to the sepulcher."[11]

Peter then lifted the head of the body and began to sing: "Israel has come out of Egypt, Alleluia."[12] And with John carrying the palm before the bier, the apostles bore the body of Mary, singing songs of praise together with Peter.

As they were going, a cloud appeared, in form a circle such as sometimes covers the face of the moon. And a host of angels was in the cloud singing with the apostles until the sweetness of the sound filled the whole city. And when the people heard it, they came out of their houses—about fifteen thousand in all—and were amazed at the sound. Nor could they tell where it was coming from, until a voice said, "Mary has gone from the body." Then the people looked and saw the bier passing by, crowned with the glory of God, and they heard the apostles singing with voices both sweet and loud.

But the chief priest[13] was enraged at the sight of the procession and pushed his way forward, intending to overturn the bier and put a stop to the display. But when his hands touched the bier, they withered up to the elbows and became like the bones of a dead man and cleaved to the bier. And he was dragged along the road in torment as the apostles continued on their way to the sepulcher. Still there were scoffers in the crowd who had sided with the priest, and the angels in the clouds struck them blind for their unbelief.[14]

The priest cried out, "Peter, I am in great pain. Remember that once I saved your skin: when the woman in the judgment hall recognized you as a disciple of Jesus, I did not torment you."[15]

And Peter said, "I am not the one who can save you. If you are willing to believe in your heart that Jesus Christ is Lord and that the woman who rests here on the bier is the one who gave birth to the Lord, and that she was a virgin still after his birth, then the Lord's mercy will find you."

The high priest said in his agony, "How can we not believe? But what are we to do about it? The Enemy of Mankind has blinded us. Shame covers our faces for we cried out against the Christ and we did not confess God's mighty works in him when we should have done. We are cursed in our unbelief."

But Peter looked at the priest and said, "Not so: the curse is a curse on those who continue in their unbelief. To those who will turn to Christ no mercy is denied."

And the priest said at last, "Peter, I believe everything that you have said to me; and I beg you, ask the Lord's forgiveness for my sake, since I am about to die."

Peter made the bier stand still and said to the high priest: "If you do believe in the Lord Jesus Christ with your heart, then your hands shall be freed from this bier."

And no sooner had Peter said this than the man's hands were freed and he stood on his feet. But his arms were still like those of a dead man, all bone and no flesh, so Peter said to him, "Go, now: stand near to the body of the holy mother and kiss the bed, and say, 'I believe in God and in the son of God, born of this woman. I believe in Jesus Christ and in everything spoken to me by his apostle.'"

The priest then came close to the bier and kissed it, and said everything that Peter had commanded him to say. And as soon as it was done, his arms were healed. And the priest began to sing God's praises with the apostles, and to teach the people from the books of Moses all the testimonies to Christ—so eloquently that the apostles marveled at his wisdom and began to weep for joy.

When Peter saw the mercy of God he said to the priest, "Now take this palm and lift it among the people in the city who were blinded by the angel; touch their eyes with it and they will be healed, provided they believe in the Lord Jesus Christ. But those who will not believe shall continue in their blindness."

So the priest entered the city and found people distressed and stricken: "We are like the men of Sodom," they wailed, "we are punished by God for our wickedness."

But the high priest spoke to them movingly of the mercy of Christ and how he had been healed from his affliction, and the people believed him. Then he touched their eyes with the palm which Peter had given him, and they received back their sight. But some only said they believed, when they really did not, and those who were hardened to the news of salvation died when the priest touched their eyes.

Meanwhile the apostles came with the bier to the Valley of Josaphat, which the Lord had showed them. There they found the tomb, and laid Mary in it and sealed the door. Then they sat down at the tomb to keep watch in case anyone should think to steal the body of the holy mother of the Lord from the sepulcher.[16]

And when they had positioned themselves outside the tomb, the Lord Jesus Christ came to them and said, "Peace be to you." And his brightness flashed everywhere around them. They answered him, "Have mercy upon us, O Lord; you are our hope."

Then Jesus spoke to them and said, "Before I ascended to the Father I promised you that my followers would one day sit on twelve thrones to judge the twelve tribes of Israel. This woman was chosen from among the twelve tribes to be the one in whom the godhead itself would dwell. What shall be done with her?"

Peter said, "Lord, you know all things; you see all things since before the beginning of the world. You chose this woman to be the mother of God; and you chose us to be your followers. She is your true handmaiden, your immaculate chamber. If through your grace it is your will, then it seems good to your servants here that you should take this woman's body with you to dwell with you in eternal glory, as you yourself were raised up to sit at the right hand of your father."

And Jesus smiled and said, "This is what I want."

And he commanded Micha-el the archangel to release the soul of Mary from the silken purse in which it had been sealed, and Micha-el came and broke the seal on the sepulcher and rolled back the stone. Then the Lord said, "Mary, rise up, my beloved mother. You did not know sin during your life, nor shall your body know corruption after death."

And Mary got up from the bier and came to Jesus and fell at his feet to worship him. And she said, "Lord, there is no way for me to repay you for the many favors I have received from your hand. Let your name be blessed forever, redeemer of the world and king of Israel."

The Lord kissed her and then said to his apostles, "Draw near to me." He kissed each one in turn, then spoke to them a last time: "Peace be to all of you: as I am with you now, so I shall always be with you until the end of the world." Then he departed and immediately the angels surrounded Mary in order to lift her into paradise after her son.

Thomas saw the body being lifted up and cried out to her,[17] "Mary, mother of God, make one of Christ's servants sure of your mercy." And immediately the linen in which the apostles had wrapped the body of Mary fell down from the clouds and Thomas took it and ran to join the others in the Valley of Josaphat, since he had not been among those who witnessed the events at the tomb.[18] And Peter said to him, "You who were always small in faith, what do you think now?" And he showed Thomas the empty tomb where the body of Mary had been laid. And Thomas showed the apostles the linen that had fallen from the heavens, and all praised God together.

# Epilogues

## THE HYMN OF THE PEARL[1]

### *A Hymn of the Christ Child in Heaven*

When I was a child
in the palace of my father,
reposing in the abundance of those who loved me,
from the east, my homeland, my parents sent me.

I was provisioned from their treasure-horde
with a load incomparable,
    great things, little things,
    things I alone might bear.

For gold from Gilead is my burden
and the treasure-silver of Gazzak

and Chalcedonian stone of India,
and of the land of Kushan, pearls.
They armed me with gray adamant, harder than iron;
and they took from me a garment beset with gemstones,
spangled with gold,
because they loved me.

In ordinary dress they sent me.

Then my own father made compact with me
and he inscribed it on my understanding,
saying: Forget not this, forget not
that if you go into Egypt
and return from there with the one pearl
kept in the middle of a sea,
guarded by the hungry serpent,
then you will earn the right again
to put on the garment set with gems,
and the princely robes you leave behind.
You will become with your brother
heir to my kingdom.

So I came out of the East,
guided by two guides,
along a road both thorny and fearsome:
and I was like a child, innocent of its ways.
I passed by the archons of Maishan,
the trading post of the eastern merchants;
I reached the land of the Babylonians,
and reached beyond.

But when I entered Egypt,
my two guides who traveled with me
deserted me.

So I made straightaway for the serpent's lair
and I stayed close by his hole,
waiting for him to snore,
that I might snatch away the precious pearl.

I was alone;
I changed my aspect
and seemed an alien to my own people.[2]

And I saw my kinsman from the East,
a son of princes, a boy of grace and beauty,
an anointed one.
And he came to stay with me.

He stayed with me and I made him
an heir of my treasure
and a wayfarer on my journey.
But I charged him: Beware of the Egyptians
with their unclean ways.

Then I became like one of them,
as not to seem a stranger to them,
or to seem like someone from above,
who had come to take the pearl,
and so that the Egyptians
would not awaken the serpent.

But they learned of my coming
by guile, and knew that I was from above;
and they mixed a potion for me in my food,
and I ate it.

And I forgot that I was the son
of a king, and became a servant
of their king.

And I forgot the pearl
for which my father had sent me,
and I fell into a deep sleep.

But my father saw it on high
and grieved for my servitude:
A council was called
to which all the kings of the East
were invited, the king of Parthia,
the great kings of the East.
And they resolved that
I should not be forsaken in Egypt.

And this is what they wrote,
this is what the kings sent to me:

From your father, the king of kings,
and your mother, Queen of the East,
and your brother who sits next to our throne:
    Peace.

Rise up and awaken out of sleep in Egypt.
Listen to the words of the letter:
Remember that you are a king and son of kings.
You have become a slave in Egypt.
Remember: the pearl for which you were sent into Egypt.
Remember: your princely garment beset with gems
and the glorious robes you will wear.
Your name is in the Book of Life,
and with your brother, next to us, you
shall inherit the kingdom.

Then my father the king
of kings sealed the letter
with his right hand,

and, lest the evil ones
—the Babylonians and demons—
tried to keep it from me,
he sent it strapped to the wings of an eagle,
the prince of the air.

The eagle flew and lighted near to me,
and then it spoke.
I awoke from my sleep,
sat up, and opened and read,
and remembered the letters
which were inscribed on my heart:
how I was the son of kings,
and how my proper station was above.
I remembered the pearl, for which
I had been sent into Egypt,
and I came with power against the awful monster,
the serpent who guarded the gem.
I came against him.
I overcame him by naming
my Father's name on his head,
and the name of my brother,
and the name of my mother, Queen of the East.

I snatched the pearl and I ascended,
turning back to my father's house.
I stripped off the filthy garment
and left it behind in the the land of Egypt
and turned my face again toward the East,
toward my homeland.

The letter which had awakened me from slavery
spoke, as though it had a voice,
and it guided me with a brightness

and kept the silken garment promised me
by my father always in front of my eyes.

It caused me to speed, encouraged me onward,
And I passed by Labyrinthus,
Babylon over my left shoulder,
and came to Maishan the Great, that lies
on the sea. The jeweled robe
that my father had stripped from me,
the royal mantle in which I was clad,
had been sent to Hyrcania, and lay
in the hands of those most faithful.

I had forgotten its dazzling whiteness
for I was still a child when I had left it
in the palace of my father. Suddenly,
I saw the garment reflect me like a mirror:
I saw myself in it, it in me:
we that had been divided were once again
made into one, into one form.
The treasure-keepers that brought it to me,
who were two, displayed on their heads
one royal seal. They clutched money in their hands
and used it to pay me a price, and the garment,
dazzling in many colors, now shining with
gold, stones, and pearls, shone now in the heights.

The likeness of the King of kings
shone through
all of it—
shining with the brightness of sapphires.

The motion of Knowledge was beginning now,
and the garment was ready to speak:

and it did speak, as though it were many voices,
and it said:
I AM HE AND I AM OF HIM
who is more marvelous than any man.
    I was reared by the Father himself.
    I know his true nature.
    I know His motions.
And as it spun, its movement sped toward me
and entered me, and its impulse spread
over me.
It reached out and took me,
and I yearned to be taken by it.
I stretched forth for it to enter me,
and made myself its fit dwelling place.
I adorned myself in its colors
and was beautiful in my adornment.

When I had put it on, I was lifted
into the place of peace, greeting, and homage:
I bowed my head and worshiped
the Father who sent the raiment to me.

I had been obedient
to the commandments of my Father.
He was obedient to the Promise he had made.
At the doors of his palace
which was In the Beginning,
I mingled with the worthies
of his house. He rejoiced for my return,
and he took me into his mansion.

All his servants praise my father
with angelic voices:

And the promise is a promise of kingship;
the promise to abide with the King—
I, my treasures, my pearl.


# THE PHILIPPIAN INCARNATION HYMN[3]


He always had the nature of God
    but did not think that by force
he should remain God's equal.

Instead of this, by his obedience,
    he gave up all that he had
taking the nature of a servant.
He became Man,
he put on the form of humanity.

He humbled himself greatly
and walked the way of obedience,
even to death—
the death of the cross.

And for this God mightily raised Him,
to the highest place above
and has cloaked him in the Name
that is above all names.

So that at Jesus' name
all powers in heaven
and in the world below
fall on their knees.

And all proclaim as one:

Jesus Christ is Lord,
To the glory of the Father.


# A MISCELLANY OF NATIVITY HYMNS[4]


### *Quem Vidistis Pastores?*


Speak, shepherds:
What have you seen?
What has appeared below,
Tell us.

"We saw a child,
choirs of angels
praising the Lord. Alleluia."

What have you seen, shepherds?

"The mother gave birth
to the king named Eternal,
blending motherhood sweet
with God-made virginity.
Her equal is not known,
nor ever will be seen, Alleluia."

And a man of light
said to herdsmen:

"I bring you God's news

to enjoy:
this is the day
of the Savior's birth, Alleluia."

A heavenly army, a thousand ranks,
stood with the angel
praising God and saying,
"Glory to Him in highest heaven;
peace to the righteous ones below:

"A child is born this day,
Mighty God he is named.

"God who spoke variously
through prophets
and through the fathers
has last of all
spoken through the Son
whom he made the heir of all things,
by whom he made the world."


### A Solis Ortus Cardine


Let all the world
from East to West
Sing of Christ,
the King, the Virgin's Son.

The blessed maker of the world
snatched servant's garb
to liberate the captives,

and capture what was lost.

Heavenly breath
enters the chaste mother
and a virgin's womb keeps a secret
she could never breathe.

The home of her sweet womb
becomes instantly God's Temple:
she, undefiled, without a man,
conceives the Son of Man.

She births the one that Gabriel
sang, that John still
in his mother's womb leaped
to be near.

Hay was his bed,
his shelter an ox-stall:
the child who gives sparrows their fill
was fed with little milk.

An angel choir praised God
in his glory.
The Shepherd of all
smiles at the shepherds.

## Jesu Redemptor Omnium

Jesus all-redeemer:
Before the light was made

you were in the splendor
of the mighty Father.

Hear, O Father's Sun
and Beauty, our frail hope
and hear your servants
throughout creation:

This day comes round
to tell the news that you
have come, salvation-bringer,
Father's sole-begotten.

You write a new thing:
heaven and earth, the seas,
the beasts who prowl your world
Greet you with a song.

Remember at your birth
you took from Mary's womb
our body's form, God-Word
made flesh.

O secret exchange!
the Creator of man
became a man and
through the Virgin Mother
godded us.

In the bush Moses saw
burning, not burnt,
we see her virginity
marvelously preserved:
the Mother of God
who helps the voyagers.

## *O Sola Magnarum Urbium*


Bethlehem, greater than great
cities, blessed to bring
to birth in the flesh
the heaven-sent leader of salvation:

Before the daystar,
before the ages,
he was begotten, and this day
he appears to the world,

Jerusalem's Light has come,
its sun is shining,
tribes are marching
under its light.

And a star beautifully bright
outshines this sun,
saying, "God has come
in earth's flesh for
earth's redemption."

And with eastern pomp
Magi bring gifts, bowing low
near his manger:
incense, myrrh, and royal gold.

The gold-gift means
he is king, and the sweet
smelling incense discloses
he is God. The resin
myrrh foretells his tomb.

The kings of Tharsis
and the Isles offer gifts,
the kings of Arabia and Saba
bring tribute. All from Saba
shall come bearing gold and
frankincense, announcing he is Lord.


### *Jacob Autem Genuit*


Jacob was the father of Joseph,
husband of Mary, of whom
was born Jesus called the Christ.

In a dream
a messenger of God
said, "Joseph, do not fear
to take Mary as a wife. What
is in her, son of David,
is from the Holy Spirit."

Shepherds came quickly
and found Mary, Joseph,
and, in a manger, the babe.

Entering the house
the magi found the child
with Mary, his mother,

And his father and mother
wondered at the God-breathed things
spoken about him.

158

## *O Lux Beata Caelitum*

Shining of sky,
earth's highest hope,
the baby Jesus
greeted his mother Mary
at birth with the smile
of family love.

And Mary full of grace,
chosen to nurse the babe
at her shining breast,
feeds and kisses him,

And Joseph good man,
chosen of old from the Jews
to guard and protect Mary,
dutifully called "Father"
by the God-child—

Listen to the prayers
we pray at your altars:
you who came from Jesse's
line for man's salvation.

## *Sacra Iam Splendent*

The holy temples reflect
the light of the lamps

shining. The altar
is greened and smoking censers
send perfumed homage.

This is the right time
to sing the royal lineage
of the Father's Son,
the time to sing David's house
and the famous men of old:

But better to sing a lower thing,
a lowly house at Nazareth
and its mean condition:
sweeter to tell in song
Jesus' hidden life.

The angel speaks, the child
goes home, the hard path
hurts its feet: an exile
from the Nile banks, he slumbers
safe under his father's roof.

He grows, his radiance
hidden, learned in Joseph's craft,
he yields to be Joseph's
sweet companion
and to work the wood.

"Let sweat bathe my
limbs," he says, "before my body
runs with blood. Let humility
and toil help pay the price
of wiping clean the stain of earth."

Mary, mother,

sits beside her son,
the wife beside her husband,
happy in this:
that her presence lifts
the aching burden of work.


## *O Gente Felix Hospita*


O gentle Nazareth!
the home of people so rare,
the golden sun sees everything
but nothing so wonderful,
so holy as the house of Joseph.

Messengers flock constantly
from heaven's court
to spy, to steal the scent
of divinity's own perfume.

With what skill, what care
Jesus bends to Joseph's whims;
with what joy Mary
savors her motherhood.

Joseph stays near
to shoulder a burden;
and Jesus stands silently
between, tightening the bond
of love between them.

## Crudelis Herodes

Wicked Herod! Do you fear
God's kingly coming?
Why? For the maker of heaven
does not destroy earth's kingdoms.

Magi follow a star
along their way, seeking
the Light by its light;
their incense owns him
to be God.

Heaven's lamb has now
been washed in Jordan's water,
washing us of sins
that were not his.

And now, the sign:
a new thing happens—water jars
redden at a word, bidden
to be wine, completely changed.

Glory to you, Jesus,
who would not stay hidden;
and glory to the Father
and to the loving spirit
through ages without end,

Amen.

# IGNATIUS OF ANTIOCH ON THE NATIVITY

And the virginity of Mary and her giving birth were hidden from the prince of this world, as was also the death of the Lord. Three mysteries of a cry which were wrought in the stillness of God. How then was he manifested to the world? A star shone in heaven beyond all the stars, and its light was unspeakable and its newness caused astonishment, and all the other stars, with the sun and moon, gathered in chorus around this star, and it far exceeded them in all its light; and there was perplexity, whence came this new thing so unlike them.

By this, all magic was dissolved and every bond of wickedness vanished away, ignorance was removed, and the old kingdom was destroyed, for God was manifest as man for the newness of eternal life, and that which had been prepared by God received its beginning. Hence all things were disturbed, because the abolition of death was being planned.[5]

# THE APOCRYPHAL INFANCY TRADITION IN ISLAM[6]

[*Surah* 3.33–60]

God chose Adam, Noah, the house of Abraham, and the house of 'Imran before all creatures in a line of continuous descent. God hears and knows.

When the wife of 'Imran [Joachim] said, "Lord, I vow to your service my unborn child: accept my offering. For you see and know all things."

When she gave birth to her daughter she said, "Lord, a daughter is born to me." God was well aware what the child was. A female birth is not the same as a male. "I have named her Mary. I entrust her into your protection and her seed after her from the malice of Satan."

Her Lord received her with gracious favor and under His hand she grew into a goodly child. The Lord gave her into the care of Zechariah.

Every time Zechariah entered the sanctuary he found her supplied with food. "Mary," he said, "how do you come to have this food?" "It is God's providence," she replied. "For God gives without stint to whomever he wills."

Then Zechariah prayed, "Lord, hearer of prayer, grant me at your hand a blessed offspring." As he was standing in the sanctuary in the act of prayer angels called to him and said, "God, confirming his word, brings you happy news. It is about John, a prince of men and chaste, a prophet numbered with the righteous." "Lord," said Zechariah, "how shall I have a son when I am now an old man and my wife is barren?" "God brings about what he wills: that is how it will be."

Then Zechariah said, "Lord, let me have a sign." "Your sign,"

[God] said, "will be that for three days you will speak to no one except by gestures. Celebrate the praise of your Lord evening and morning and remember him often."

And the angels said, "Mary, God has chosen you. Truly he has chosen you above all women everywhere. Mary, be obedient to your Lord, prostrate yourself in worship and join yourself with those who pray."

This is a narrative of things concealed which we have given you to know. For you were not present when they cast their lots over who should have the care of Mary, and you were not on hand when they vied for the custody of her.

To Mary the angels said: "Mary, God gives you glad news of a word from him. His name is the Messiah Jesus, son of Mary. Eminent will he be in this world and in the age to come, and he will have his place among those who are brought near to God's throne. He will speak to men in the cradle, and in his mature years he will be among the righteous."

Mary said, "Lord, how will I bear a son when no man has known me?" [The angel] replied, "The will of God is so, for he creates as he wills. When his purpose is decreed he only says, 'Be!' and it is. God will teach him the scripture, the wisdom, the Torah, and the Gospel, making him a messenger to the people of Israel, to whom he will say, "I have come to you with a sign from the Lord. Out of clay I will shape for you the form of a bird, and as I breathe on it it will become one, by God's authority. Also I will heal the blind and the leper and bring the dead to life, by God's authority. I will bring you word of what to eat and what to hold in store in your houses. Truly that will constitute a sign for you, if you are minded to believe. I come confirming the truth that you have already in your possession, namely the Torah, and to authorize for you certain things that were hitherto forbidden. I am here among you with a sign from your Lord. Then hold God in awe and be obedient to me, God is my Lord and your Lord: therefore serve him. This is the straight path. . . ."

*[Surah 19.1–36]*

The mercy of your Lord to his servant Zechariah is here recalled. In the secret of his heart he entreated his Lord saying, "Lord, I am a feeble old man with snow white hair. Yet never when I called on you, Lord, have I been left forlorn. I have a fear as to my kinsfolk after my decease, and my wife is childless. Grant me, I pray, an heir at your hand who will enter on my inheritance and that of Jacob's family also. Let him be a man to please you, Lord."

"Zechariah," came the answer, "We give you glad news of a son, John his name, a name which we have not before now bestowed on any one." He said, "My Lord, how shall a son be mine when my wife is barren and I as old and decrepit as I am?" His Lord replied: "It shall be so—Your Lord's word for it. It is no hard thing. When you yourself long ago were nonexistent, I brought you into being."

"My Lord," said Zechariah, "grant me a sign." "The sign for you," his Lord answered, "is that for three whole days you will not be able to speak."

So he emerged from the sanctuary to his people and indicated to them that should engage morning and evening in praise to God. To John when he was still a child we gave authority, saying, "John, lay hold upon the Book with all your strength." Tenderness, too, and purity, we granted him. He was devout and dutiful to his parents, and never overbearing or contentious. Blessed be he on the day of his birth and the day of his death and the day when he is raised again to life.

Recall too in the Book how it was with Mary when she withdrew from her family to a place eastward where she was hidden from them behind a curtain. There we sent to her our spirit who came to her in comely form. "I take refuge from you in the All-Merciful," she cried. "If you are a man of honor. . . ." But her words were lost as he said, "I am sent from your Lord. I will give you a son, a pure boy, he says to you."

Mary said, "How shall a son be mine when no man has ever known me, nor have I ever been unchaste?" "So it shall be," he said. "Your Lord's word is, 'It is easy for me, and we shall make him a sign to humanity and a token of our mercy.' What is decreed is utterly sure."

So, she became pregnant and withdrew to a remote spot, where pangs of travail came upon her beside a palm tree. And she cried, "Would I had died before now, and disappeared without a trace!" There came a voice from below the tree: "Be not sad. See, there is a stream beneath you—God's doing for you. Shake the trunk of the palm tree and fresh ripe dates will drop down around you. Eat and drink and take heart. If anyone accosts you, all you have to say is: 'I am under a vow to the all-merciful to fast and this day, I hold converse with nobody.' "

Then she brought the child in her arms to her family: they said to her, "Mary, for shame! Whatever have you done? Sister of Aaron, your father was no profligate, nor was your mother a loose woman!" Whereupon she simply turned their glances in the child's direction, and they retorted: "How shall we address words to a child in the cradle?" And the child said: "I am the servant of God. He has given me the Book and appointed me a prophet, and he has made me blessed wherever I am. He has commanded me to pray and to do alms all my life long, and to be dutiful to my mother. What belongs to the arrogant and the wretched has no place in his will for me. Blessed am I in the day of my birth, my day of death, and my day of resurrection to life."

Such was Jesus, son of Mary—the true word about him which is a matter of doubt among [Christians]. It is not for God to adopt a son. All praise be his. . . .

# Appendix

## The Family of Jesus

*James*

The fourth-century church historian Eusebius quotes the following from a late second-century writer named Hegesippus who wrote five books of memoirs, and whom Eusebius identifies as "belonging to the generation after the apostles":

"The charge of the church passed to James, the brother of the Lord, together with the apostles. He was called 'the just' by all men from the Lord's time to our own, since many are called James, but he was holy from his mother's womb. He drank no wine or strong drink nor did he eat flesh; no razor went upon his head; he did not anoint himself with oil, and he did not go to the baths. He alone was allowed to enter into the sanctuary; for he did not wear wool but linen, and he used to enter alone into the temple and be found kneeling and praying for forgiveness for the people, so that his knees grew hard

169

like a camel's because of his constant worship of God, kneeling and asking forgiveness for the people.

"So from excessive righteousness he was called 'the just,' or *oblias* in Greek, 'Rampart of the People and righteousness,' as the prophets declare concerning him. Thus some of the seven sects among the people who were described before me . . . inquired of him what was the 'gate of Jesus,' and he said he was the savior.

"Owing to this some believed that Jesus was the Christ. The sects mentioned above did not believe either in resurrection or in one who shall come to reward each according to his deeds, but as many as believed did so because of James. Now since many even of the rulers believed, there was a tumult of the Jews and the scribes and the Pharisees saying that the whole people was in danger of looking for Jesus as the Christ. So they assembled and said to James, 'We beseech you to restrain the people since they are straying after Jesus as though he were the Messiah. We beseech you to persuade concerning Jesus all who come for the day of Passover, for all obey you. Therefore, stand on the battlement of the temple that you may be clearly visible on high, and that your words may be audible to all the people, for because of the Passover all the tribes, with the Gentiles also, have come together.'

"So the scribes and the Pharisees mentioned before made James stand on the battlement of the temple and they cried out to him and said, 'O just one, to whom we all owe obedience, since the people are straying after Jesus who was crucified, tell us, What is the gate of Jesus?' And he answered with a loud voice, 'Why do you ask me concerning the son of man? He is sitting in heaven on the right hand of the great power, and he will come on the clouds of heaven.' And many were convinced and confessed at the testimony of James, and said, 'Hosanna to the Son of David.'

"Then again the same scribes and Pharisees said to one another, 'We did wrong to provide Jesus with such testimony, but let us go up and throw him down that they may be afraid and not believe him.' And they cried out and said, 'Oh, oh, even the just one erred.' And they fulfilled the scripture written in Isaiah, 'Let us take the just man for he is unprofitable to us. Yet they shall eat the fruit of their works.' So they went up and threw down the just, and they said to one another, 'Let us stone James the Just,' and they began to stone him since the fall had not killed him, but he turned and knelt, saying, 'I beseech thee, O Lord, God and Father, forgive them, for they know not what they do.'

"And while they were thus stoning him, one of the priests of the sons of Rechab, the son of Rechabim, . . . cried out saying 'Stop, what are you doing? The Just is praying for you.' And a certain man among them, one of the landrymen, took the club with which he used to beat out the clothes and hit the Just on the head, and so he suffered martyrdom. And they buried him on the spot by the temple, and his gravestone still remains by the temple. . . ." (Eusebius, *Ecclesiastical History* 2.23.4–18)

## Jude

Under the emperor Domitian (51–96 C.E.) certain parties complained about the descendants of Jude, who were claiming a relationship through David's line to the Messiah. Eusebius again uses as his source the second-century writer Hegesippus (*Ecclesiastical History* 3.20.1–6):

"An ancient story goes that some heretics accused the grandsons of Jude who is said to have been the brother, according to the flesh, of the savior, saying that they were of the family of David and related to Christ himself; writes Hegesippus, 'Now there still survived of the family of the Lord grandsons of Jude who was said to have been his brother according to the flesh, and they were related as being of the family of David.'

"These the officer brought to Domitian Caesar, for like Herod he was afraid of the coming of the Christ. He asked them if they were of the house of David and they admitted it. Then he asked them how much property they had or how much money they controlled and they said that all they possessed was nine thousand denarii between them. . . . They then showed him their hands adducing as testimony of their labor the hardness of their bodies and the tough skin which had been embossed on their hands from their incessant work. They were asked concerning the Christ and his kingdom, its nature, origin and time of appearance, and explained that it was neither of the world nor earthly but heavenly and angelic. . . . At this Domitian did not condemn them at all, but despised them as simple folk, released them, and decreed an end to persecution against the church. But when they were released they were the leaders of the churches, both for their testimony and for their relation to the Lord and remained alive in the peace which ensued until Trajan."

## Cleopas

According to Hegisippus, Joseph had a brother names Clopas or Cleopas, a name which is also mentioned in John 19.25. The same writer says that Cleopas' son, Simeon (a legal cousin of Jesus and of James) was appointed by unanimous decision to head the Jerusalem church after the death of James. Between Domitian and Trajan (see above) the church is supposed to have enjoyed relative peace, until Simeon was brought up on charges before the governor

Atticus as a Christian "heretic." He was tortured for several days and finally crucified; his bravery in the face of suffering is said to have inspired even Atticus.

## *Mary of Cleopas*

Mentioned in John 19.25 as standing beneath the cross with other women is, in the ancient Sahidic tradition, the daughter (sometimes the wife) of Cleopas. Matthew 27.56 and Mark 15.40 recount a second Mary, other than Mary the Mother of Jesus and Mary Magdalene. St. Jerome presents an alternative; while not explaining the relationship of Mary to Cleopas, she thinks of this second Mary as the sister of Mary, mother of Jesus (cf. John 19.25). That the two sisters both would have been named Mary, in this case, does not especially bother Jerome. A further complication occurs if we take Mary of Cleopas as the daughter rather than the wife of Cleopas; in this case, Cleopas becomes the father of the two Marys (rather than Joachim), and in certain gospel fragments from upper Egypt as well as in the Gospel of the Pseudo-Matthew, it is said that God gave Mary of Cleopas as a consolation to *Cleopas* and Anna in exchange for their giving the first Mary to the temple as a gift to God.

## *Salome*

Known from Mark 15.41 as one of the women watching the crucifixion at a distance, Salome is also the name given to Joseph's first wife and a kinswoman of Mary and Elizabeth. Matthew 27.56 appears to identify her as the mother of James and John, the sons of Zebedee, and some of the church fathers identified her as the sister of Mary on the basis of John 19.25.

# Endnotes

## Introduction

1. *The Old Testament Pseudepigrapha*, 2 vols., ed. J. H. Charlesworth (New York: Doubleday, 1983–85). On the Dead Sea Scrolls, see especially the discussion of James C. VanderKam, *The Dead Sea Scrolls Today* (Grand Rapids, Mich.: Eerdmans, 1994). A still serviceable work is Geza Vermes's *The Dead Sea Scrolls in English* (Harmondsworth: Penguin, 3rd ed., 1987).

2. On recent work in what is often called "social scientific" or contextual biblical study, see the remarks of David M. May, *Social Scientific Criticism of the New Testament* (Macon, Ga.: Mercer University Press, 1991).

3. Athanasius's festal letter (xxxix) of 367 is usually understood as the climax of a long process of canon-building and inventory. Greek text with translation in A. Souter, *The Text and Canon of the New Testament* (London: Duckworth, 1954), pp. 196–98.

4. Irenaeus, *Against Heresies* 3.17.4.

5. Controversy over the Book of Revelation, the Epistle to the Hebrews, and some of the later epistles continued for centuries. The Syrian church continued to use a harmonization of the gospels (the Diatessaron) until the fifth century.

6. See M. R. James, *The Apocryphal New Testament* (Oxford: Oxford University Press, 1928, elsewhere cited as NTA), p. xiv. James failed to mention that the term ἀπόκρυφος was used in the Greek church from the earliest period simply to mean a work not read in a *public* service (i.e., for public reading). No stigma was attached to such a work; it was simply not for public dissemination. In the Latin church a similar distinction was made between the *apocryphae,* or secret books, and the *manifesti* or *vulgati* (those used in public services). See Souter, *Text and Canon,* p. 145.

7. Irenaeus, *Against Heresies* 3.2.2.

8. Popular description of the discovery of this cache of material is provided in Elaine Pagels, *The Gnostic Gospels* (New York: Random House, 1979), and by Bentley Layton, *The Gnostic Scriptures* (London: SCM, 1987), esp. pp.i–xxvii.

9. I will need to explain this assertion for those who will be aware that gnostic compositions such as the *Gospel of Thomas* and the *Gospel of Philip* do in fact capitalize on the warrant of apostolic authority. My point is that the historical ascription is gratuitous: the content of a gnostic gospel is "authoritative," insofar as that concept played any role at all, not because of the historical status of its writer but because the content is revealed. In *Thomas,* for example, the incipit shows that it is less the "author's" apostolic status that confers authority than the fact that his record is of "secret sayings." On gnostic complexity see K. Rudolph, *Gnosis* (San Francisco: Harper and Row, 1977), pp. 67–171.

10. Irenaeus, *Against Heresies* 3.4.1.

11. See on the question of transmission "Form und traditionsgeschichtliche Fragen," in H. Koester, *Einführung in das Neue Testament* (Berlin: Walter de Gruyter, 1980), pp. 492–503.

12. James, NTA, xii.

13. A thorough examination of the evidence is Jane Schaberg's *The Illegitimacy of Jesus* (San Francisco: Harper and Row, 1987).

14. To cite one famous example, the *Book of James* (*Protevangelium*), written in the early second century (>150 C.E.) was popular with Ebionite (Jewish) Christians, the Greek fathers, and in the Syrian, Coptic, and Armenian churches because of its high regard for Mary's virginity and the "theory" it advances that Jesus' brothers, mentioned in the gospels, were in fact Joseph's sons by a previous marriage. Condemnation of the gospel came from Jerome, who argued that the brothers were, in fact, cousins. The church historian Eusebius (*Church History* 3.3) doubts the authenticity of 2 Peter (which was finally included in the NT canon) and notes disputes about the Epistle to the Hebrews ("which is spoken against as not being Paul's in the Roman church"), but commends the use of the Acts of Paul (apocryphal) and the *Shepherd of Hermas* as being good for instruction.

15. Acts of Pilate (Latin B) III.1

16. In fact, the *Gospel of Nicodemus* becomes a favorite source for medieval religious drama; see: K. Young, *The Drama of the Medieval Church* (Oxford, 1933), I:149–77.

17. The Acts of Pilate are almost certainly those mentioned by Justin Martyr ca. 165 when he refers pagan readers to the "Acts of Christ's trial preserved among the archives at Rome." 1 *Apology* 4.8.

18. Isaiah 7.14 in the Pentateuch (Greek OT).

19. A strong case can be made for the use of patronage in the compilation of the Acts of Pilate; see T. Mommsen, "Die Pilatusakten," *Zeitschrift für die neutestamenliche Wissenschaft* 3 (1902): 198–205. The Acts begin with a declaration that a certain Ananias, "an officer of the guard" in the reign of Theodosius, discovered a record written in Hebrew which he translated into Greek.

20. See M. D. Anderson, *Drama and Imagery in English Medieval Churches* (Cambridge: Cambridge University Press, 1963), pp. 87–177. The Antichrist, the Parable of Wise and Foolish Virgins, and the Last Judgment were other popular themes.

21. R. Morris, ed., *Cursor Mundi* (London: Early English Text Society, 1874), spelling here regularized. The poem was written in the thirteenth century in the vicinity of Durham.

22. Translation of Ps. 148.7 from the Hebrew text yields "Praise the

Lord from the earth you water spouts and ocean depths," but in the Vulgate (*"Laudate Dominum de terra dracones et omnes abyssi . . ."*) the "spouts" become snorting dragons.

23. Luther, however, uses the story of hell's harrowing in *Ein feste Berg* and was profoundly influenced by monastic renditions of apocryphal stories.

24. See Epilogues, pp. 164–67.

25. James, NTA, p. xiv.

26. The earliest evidence for this Christology comes from a Roman source, the younger Pliny's letter (X.96–7) written to the emperor Trajan ca. 112. See A. N. Sherwin-White's *The Letters of Pliny: A Historical and Social Commentary* (Oxford, 1966), pp. 691–712.

27. The doctrine of Mary's sinlessness ("immaculate conception") was solemnly promulgated in the December 8, 1854, bull *Ineffabilis Deus* by Pope Pius IX. This decree, however, was the culmination of a long history of speculation which goes back to the time of Justin Martyr, Irenaeus, Andrew of Crete, and John of Damascus. Almost all the scholastic theologians, including Bonaventure, Thomas Aquinas, and Albert, were opposed to the doctrine, arguing that Mary was conceived in the "natural" way and, as such, was not exempt from the "law of original sin" (Aquinas).

28. The belief that Mary was taken bodily to heaven (Assumption of the Virgin) was proclaimed by Pope Pius XII in the bull *Munificentissimus Deus* (1950). The sole basis for the belief are the apocryphal works "The Passing Away of Mary" and the "Obsequies of Mary," variously ascribed to John the Evangelist and Melito of Sardis. These works are condemned in the Gelasian Decree (5th century). Only in the sixth century, with St. Gregory of Tours (d. 594) do we find a strong movement in favor of the belief of the virgin's corporal "assumption" into heaven. In the eighth century, John of Damascus, repeating a story from the Council of Chalcedon (451), states that the emperor Marcian's wife Pulcheria had wanted to "possess" (own, purchase?) the body of the virgin, but was told by the bishop of Jerusalem, Juvenal, that the virgin's death had been witnessed by all the apostles and that when her tomb was later opened, it was found

empty. Dependence of this tradition on the resurrection accounts of the gospels is evident.

29. The Book of Acts also assumes James's authority: cf. Acts 12, 15; and according to an ancient tradition (cf. 1 Cor. 15.7; Gal. 1.19), he was granted a special appearance of the risen Jesus and became "caliph" or leader of the Jerusalem church. As reported by Eusebius (*Eccles. History*, 2.23), James was the first "bishop" of Jerusalem and was put to death by the Sanhedrin in 62 C.E. (thus, the Christian writer Hegesippus).

30. On Aelred's use of the New Testament apocrypha, see G. Webb and A. Walker, *On Jesus at Twelve Years Old* (London, 1956).

31. Proverbs 7.4–5; 3.13–18; James 3.17.

# THE TEXTS

## III. *The History of the Virgin*

1. On the confusion of Mary the mother of Jesus and the "other" Marys in the gospel tradition, including Mary Magdalene (= Mary of Magdala), see my discussion in *Jesus Outside the Gospels* (Amherst, N.Y.: Prometheus Books, 1984), pp. 4–23. Discussion by A. Meyer and W. Bauer, "The Relatives of Jesus," in Hennecke-Schneemelcher, NTA, I:418–32.

2. See Numbers 26.9–11.

## V. *The Visit and Trial*

1. The "water of bitterness" is prescribed in Num. 5.17 for use in revealing the guilt or innocence of a woman accused of adultery by her husband in the absence of witnesses, and seems to have been used only in cases when the woman was pregnant. After swearing an oath of innocence and making a cereal offering of barley meal, the priest wrote an imprecation into a book and washed it out into the water. The potion was then offered to the woman who was told the curse would become effective if she was guilty. If innocent, the curse became inoperative. Joseph's being made to drink the water is an embellishment designed to underscore his own righteousness in refusing to charge Mary with the sin of adultery.

## VII. *The Nativity of Jesus, Called the Christ*

1. The two nations are Israel, weeping for its rejection of the messiah, and Rome, or the gentiles, laughing to celebrate their acceptance by God.

## XI. *The Jealousy of a King*

1. The reason for the mangering of the infant in Luke 2.7 ("because there was no space at the inn") seems to be a pious fiction designed to seclude the older tradition, preserved in the apocryphal books, that Mary was trying to disguise her child as a young animal and thereby to save his life. Luke does preserve the story of Herod's rage at the coming of the magician-spies; similarly, Matthew does not tell the story of the manger (cf.

Matt. 1.25). The obvious source of the story, including the tradition of the cave, is the hiding of the infant Zeus in a cave at Lyktos: Hesiod, *Theogony* 480ff. The myth is Cretan in origin. The tale of the shepherds can be traced to the tradition that Zeus was reared among the shepherds of Mount Ida.

2. The gruesome death of Herod, described in detail by Josephus in *The Antiquities* 17.6.5, was seen by the Jews as a divine verdict on his idolatrous rule and by the Christian interpreters as punishment for his attempts to locate and murder the "rightful" King of the Jews.

3. On the *Book of James* also commonly known as the *Protevangelium*, see H. R. Smid, *Protevangelium Jacobi: A Commentary* (Assen: Apocrypha Novi Testamenti 1, 1965); Greek text in Tischendorf: 1876, 1–50; and see bibliographical note, pp. 193–94. The gospel is often assigned to a Jewish-Christian writer working in the early second century who was himself a compiler of ancient traditions: Justin, Clement of Alexandria, and Origen cite the work.

## XII. The Child Jesus in Egypt

1. An echo of the battle to subdue Satan, "that serpent of old," in Revelation 20.1–3. The story of Chimaira (Hesiod, *Theogony* 319) and older Near Eastern myths underlie the tale. Cf. also Herakles' slaying of the Hydra.

## XIII. John and Jesus in Egypt

1. The history of the child Jesus in Egypt derives naturally enough from strands of Egyptian (Coptic and Arabic) and Syriac materials which

can be traced back at least to the 5th century (cf. Paul Peeters, *Evangiles apocryphes* [Paris, 1914], II:i.ff) from which the stories gathered here have been taken.

## *XIV. The Child Jesus in Nazareth*

1. This section is adapted largely from the infancy *Gospel of Thomas*, existing in Greek, Syriac, Arabic, and Latin versions. It was one of the most popular of the apocryphal gospels, as its linguistic dissemination suggests. It is dated by Cullmann (NTA, I:391) to the end of the second century C.E.

2. There are flashes of temper in the earliest canonical traditions as well: Mark 3.33–35 shows Jesus rejecting his family. John 2.3–4 shows him rejecting his mother's authority.

## *XVI. Jesus and the Child Zeno*

1. For an analogous theme in early Christian canonical literature, see Acts 9.36–43, Peter's raising of Tabitha from the dead. In *Thomas* the little boy's name is Zeno; in Acts the girl's name is Dorcas or Tabitha. The names provide some clue to the popularity of these stories in Greek churches of the second century.

## XVIII. The Miracle at the Well

1. Cf. John 2.1–12, which bears all the marks of an infancy story. John locates the story of the cleansing of the Temple immediately after (2.13–21), while the synoptic writers put it within the context of the passion narrative (Mark 11.15–17, pars.). This difference of location may or may not suggest that the story of the finding of the child Jesus in the Temple (Luke 2.41–51) and of the cleansing originally belonged together as a part of the infancy tradition, even though the story of the Presentation is missing in John's account.

2. In Greek mythology, the "wine miracle" of Dionysus provides an interesting analogue. See Pausanias, *Description of Greece* 6.26.1f.

## XIX. Jesus and His Father

1. Cf. Mark 4.1–8, pars., from which the tale seems to be derived.

2. The scene is a composite one but seems to derive from Mark 6.2f. and especially Luke 4.16–23, both of which passages have trappings of infancy narratives.

## XX. Jesus and James

1. Cf. Mark 16.18. The power of Jesus and the apostles led some early Christian groups, notably the Phibionites, to experiment with snake-handling.

The healing properties of venom were also recognized by the priests of the Asklepios cult, and there are significant parallels between some of the healings attributed to Asklepios in the Epidauros inscriptions (4th century B.C.E.) and those attributed to Jesus in the gospels. See "Asklepios the Healer," in H. C. Kee, *Miracle in the Early Christian World* (New Haven: Yale University Press, 1983), pp. 78–103.

2. Despite its eccentric features, Jesus' love of children or the quality of innocence exemplified by children is a recurrent theme in the infancy-tradition and seems to derive from the gospel tradition itself: Cf. Mark 10.13–16.

## XXII. *Jesus and the Doctors of the Law*

1. A variation on Luke 2.41–51, which seems to provide the basis for the "Jesus and his teachers" motif. This is by far the most irenic of the episodes and so may point to the existence of a longer narrative source (thus Cullmann) known equally by Luke and the author of the infancy *Gospel of Thomas.* In the Hermetic tradition, the young god is also said to have taught letters to Isis, an echo of which is to be found in the Lucan narrative and especially in the *Thomas* tradition that Jesus confounded his teachers with questions about the alpha and omega.

2. Luke 1.42, 51–56, adapted.

## XXIII. *The Silly Teacher*

1. A not too thinly disguised allegory in which the twelve sparrows are Israel, or perhaps rabbinical disputes over the law; Jesus—the "provider"—is the word/bread of life (John 6.25ff.), unrecognized by the silly teacher into whose lap the squabbling birds fall, making the teacher, a hypersymbol of Jewish teaching, look foolish in the eyes of his charges.

2. The story originated in disputes between Christian and Jewish teachers over the meaning of prophecy and the law. A similar case of Christian triumphalism is Justin Martyr's *Dialogue with Trypho the Jew*, written around 168.

## XXV. The Children in the Oven

1. This and the following episode are adapted from the infancy *Gospel of the Pseudo-Matthew*, here based on the text by E. Amann (Paris, 1910), pp. 272–339.

2. The speech of the women sufficiently explains the episode: the boys who refuse to play with Jesus symbolize the rejection of Jesus by the Jews (cf. John 1.12f.). The episode occurs in Arabic and Syriac versions of the infancy gospels, and in later renditions the boys are changed into pigs. The story is so widespread that it seems to rely on a very ancient tradition, perhaps being a primitive account of Jesus' acquiring his disciples in childhood.

## XXVII. The Interim

1. In Pseudo-Matthew, the other Mary is called Mary of Cleopas—a sister of Mary given to Anna and Joachim in compensation for Mary's being made a dedicated virgin of the Temple. Implicitly, this is Jesus' twelfth or thirteenth birthday, otherwise associated (Luke 2.41.ff) with the finding of Jesus in the Temple.

## XXVIII. *The Baptism*

1. Cf. 2 Kings 1.8 (the description of Elijah).

2. A number of stories in the gospels, the baptism chief among them, seem to have had their origin in the infancy legends and were later on appended to the accounts of the public ministry of Jesus. There is no time-marker in the early gospels to suggest that the baptism is not a part of the infancy tradition; perhaps it is an account of Jesus' teenage reunion with John, just arrived from Egypt. Luke's information, that Jesus was "about thirty years old when he began his work" (Luke 3.23), does not refer to the baptism, and the fact that he provides a genealogy following this information suggests a chronological break between the baptism account (Luke 3.1–22) and what follows concerning the start of the ministry.

3. Psalms 2.7 and Isaiah 42.1 are in view. Above all, however, this episode seems to have marked the acceptance or recognition by God of Jesus' sonship, an event which is here given a miraculous cast as the apotheosis of Jesus as the son of God. There are multiple "epiphanies" or revelations of Jesus' divine nature in the infancy tradition, but the baptism seems seminal. Here God reveals the completion of the mystery, begun as far back as the story of Mary's conception.

4. Deut. 8.3. The scene is reminiscent of the disputes between Jesus and his teachers: like the Tempter (or the Pharisees of the canonical tradition), Jesus is able to silence his opponents (cf. Matt. 22.46).

5. Ps. 91.11–12.

6. Deut. 6.13.

7. Cf. Mark 11.12–14, 20f. While I regard this episode, assigned by Mark to the Jerusalem period of Jesus' ministry, as being thematically related to the infancy tradition and specifically to the end of the preparation in the desert, there is no compelling reason to question Mark's placement of the tale. At the same time, its peculiarity within the Markan context has long been noticed by scholars. My own placement of it here is no more than a suggestion as to a plausible relocation.

In the Egyptian infancy tradition, Jesus causes a stubborn palm to provide fruit and water for his mother and their chattel.

8. The *Secret Gospel of Mark* (see discussion in Morton Smith, *Clement of Alexandria and a Secret Gospel of Mark* [New York, 1973]) shows Jesus raising a young man from the dead at Bethany and says that the youth six days later came to Jesus and was taught the "mystery of the Kingdom of God." The episode seems rather to belong to the apocryphal tradition than to a gnostic or (so Smith) an early Aramaic source, but probably underlies the "secret disciple" theme common to Mark 14.51 and John 11.

## XXIX. The Death of Joseph

1. Adapted from a portion of the gnostic *Pistis Sophia*, from about the third century. It occurs in a Coptic (Sahidic and Fayumic) parchment manuscript of the fourth century; text here taken from *Pistis Sophia*, ed. C. Schmidt (Copenhagen: Coptica 2, 1925). Material related to the *sophia*-tradition in the gnostic gospels discovered in 1945 at Nag Hammadi can be found in the English translation of the *Nag Hammadi Library* (New York: Harper and Row, 1977), esp. pp. 206–28. Despite its gnostic cast, it is clear that this episode has been influenced by the more "orthodox" infancy traditions of the apocryphal Christian gospels.

2. Although this point is settled doctrinally later on, there was no such agreement in the earliest literary tradition of the church and the infancy gospels reflect the unsettled state of the question.

3. In the ancient physiology, the soul passes into and out of the body through the organs used in breathing, i.e., the mouth or nostrils. Thus a person nearing death would be said to have his "soul in his throat."

4. This personification of death is typical of Near Eastern literature, where Abbaton/Thanatos is sometimes seen as a demon who resides in the underworld. Even in the Graeco-Roman context of the canonical gospels

and letters, death or the power of death is alternately personified and de-
monized, e.g., Rom. 6.10; 1 Cor. 15.26, 55f.

5. Ps. 47.8f., adapted.

6. Adapted from Ps. 141, an evening prayer for protection from the
power of death.

## XXX. The Sleep and Awakening of Mary, Virgin and Mother

1. Adapted from the *Discourse* of Theodosius, sixth-century bishop
of Alexandria. This and a volume of later accounts in Greek, Latin, Coptic, and Syriac testify to the growing popularity of devotional expansions
of the life of Mary. Because they are attempts to enhance belief in the virgin birth of the savior and her own miraculous birth, a conflation of accounts is given here.

2. Cf Matt. 28.11ff.

3. Theodosius says she was living in Jerusalem with a number of
virgins and with Peter and John; the traditions are markedly different in
details.

4. The view that the savior is especially amenable to petitions from
his mother is reflected in apocryphal texts as well as in canonical ones,
especially John 2.5, but the tradition ultimately derives from a devotional
understanding of the natural bond between a mother and son.

5. In the apocryphal tradition associated with the name of John, the
influence of the Book of Revelation is apparent. John is often the recipi-
ent of private or special revelations.

6. None of the lists of apostles present at the Virgin's bedside is very
complete or particular; some have Thomas coming late from India where
his preaching is interrupted, as he came late to be a witness to the risen
Christ (John 20.24ff.). The lists also include the names of evangelists
among the apostles, showing the relative lateness of the legends.

7. An echo of the gathering mentioned in Acts 1.14f., at which Mary is present, following the Ascension.

8. Cf. 1 Thess. 4.16f., here applied to the day of the Virgin's death as their reward for believing.

9. The implication is, of course, that the Sunday festival was the appropriate day for all of these events, notwithstanding the celebration of Christmas which was given a fixed rather than a sabbatical date from the fourth century.

10. In the Hesychast system of eastern Christian mystical theology, the uncreated light or "Light of Tabor" symbolized God's presence. The souls of the true saints were considered to be able to apprehend this light following a lifetime of spiritual purification.

11. Cf. John 19.27. The debate between Peter and John is based loosely on references in the Gospel of John to a competition between the two apostles; cf. John 20.1–8. The details of the burial are drawn mainly from the Fourth Gospel, no doubt because of the traditional association of John and Mary.

12. That is, humankind is delivered from the bondage of sin and death, Mary being the prototype among mortals. In earlier tradition only Jesus was assigned this role: Rom. 5.12–21.

13. Named Jephonias in some texts, and not identified as a priest. The story is greatly elaborated in the Latin narrative of the Pseudo-Melito.

14. As in the the gospel tradition, this polemical thrust is directed against those who reject Jesus, viz., his own people. It is not racially motivated, though the apocryphal tradition is, in general, characterized by an increase of anti-Jewish sentiment and religious stereotyping of a sort typical of its predominantly gentile composition. The canonical literature reflects late first- and early second-century ambiguities over the relationship between Judaism and Christianity; the sort of passage we find here sees official Judaism in a more villainous role.

15. Apparently a reference to John 18.17.

16. Cf. Matt. 27.62.

17. Adapted from an account attributed to Joseph of Arimathea and dependent ultimately on the story of Thomas in John 20.24–29.

18. According to a very disjointed tradition, Thomas was late in arriving from his mission in India. The geographical detail offers an opportunity to elaborate the witness of the apostle with a reputation for doubting things before he has unquestionable proof.

## Epilogues

1. This remarkable poem survives in Syriac, in Greek, and in a Coptic version from Nag Hammadi. Although it has sometimes been seen as a "gnostic" poem, it is best understood as an allegory of salvation in the wisdom tradition. It is doubtful that the poem was originally a Christian composition. Like other segments of the "hidden tradition," it seems to have been associated with the apostle Thomas (and is interpolated as a psalm of praise in the apocryphal Acts of Thomas), but its actual provenance remains uncertain. It is completely without parallel in other gnostic compositions. In the infancy tradition it constitutes a kind of "prologue in heaven," differing from the metaphysical notions of the prologue to the Fourth Gospel (John 1.1–16) in its dramatic realization of a journey through the heavenly spheres. The Hymn of the Pearl, the prologue to the Gospel of John, a section of Paul's letter to the Philippians (Phil. 2.6–11), and a section of the Pauline letter to the Christians at Colossae (1.15–20), seem to derive from a common mythological tradition. All have affinities both with the gnostic sects, especially the so-called Thomas literature, and with the Jewish wisdom tradition. According to this myth, a preexistent child (Christ, Sophia, or an Angel) descends into the created world in disguise to undo the work of the creator (thus the gnostics) or the powers of evil (thus the Christians). The descent is undertaken by stealth, the confounding of the evil powers being a central theme of the myth. In slightly later (second century) Christian tradition, the descent is transposed to the period between the crucifixion and resurrection to become a descent of Christ into hell to release the captive patriarchs. Once in the world, the

190

redeemer reveals himself to the elect or fallen, often depicted—especially in gnostic texts—as being asleep or "intoxicated," and unable to perceive the message of salvation. In the Hymn of the Pearl, the redeemer is sent to retrieve the pearl (perfect harmony?) which belongs to his Father; in Christian texts, such as John 1.1ff. and the Philippian hymn, the redemption applies to humanity and the overcoming of the satanic powers that enslave it through sin and death. Once the work is accomplished, the redeemer ascends again through the spheres or aeons, returning to his father, "divesting" himself of the disguises he has accumulated on the journey down in preparation for his enthronement and glorification. See the discussion by Layton, *Gnostic Scriptures*, pp. 366–70.

2. Cf. John 1. 10–11.

3. Phil. 2. 6–11. It is widely thought that Paul, in his letter to the Christians in Philippi, quotes an early Christian hymn. Its content, extent, and meaning are matters of some controversy, but the hymn seems to be a song of praise to the mystery of the incarnation. Whatever the source of the song, it bears a significant relationship to the story of the descent of the Logos in John 1.1–18 and to the more elaborately detailed allegory of the Hymn of the Pearl with its frankly gnostic comprehension of the divine descent and return.

4. Taken from the *editio typica* of the Divine Office of the Latin Rite. Although the canonical hours and their respective prayers were codified in the seventh century, the "pray-through-the-day" or *opus Dei* ("work of God") was known to Hippolytus of Rome in the early third century and to St. Benedict in the sixth. Latin text ed. L. Doyle (Collegeville, Minn.: Liturgical Press, 1963). These hymns show the literary tendencies of the infancy tradition as it developed within the official prayer life of the church.

5. Ignatius was bishop and head of the church in Syrian Antioch in the late first and early second centuries and was reckoned by Eusebius, the church historian, to have been appointed to the post by Euodius, an appointee of Peter the apostle. The extract comes from his Letter to the Ephesians 19.1f. and is remarkable in appearing to be independent of the canonical accounts of the nativity in the gospels of Matthew and Luke.

Text in K. Lake, *The Apostolic Fathers* (Cambridge, Mass.: Harvard University Press, 1975), from which this translation is taken.

6. Muhammad was born in Mecca about the year 570 C.E., the posthumous son of Abdullhah bin Abdul-Muttalib of the Quraysh tribe. His mother died about six years later, and the boy was reared in the family of his uncle Abu Talib. Throughout his early years, he traveled with his uncle on trading expeditions from Mecca to Syria, and it is thought that during this time he came into contact with various Arabic Christian teachers. According to Muslim tradition, in Ramadhan of the year 610, the angel Gabriel came to Muhammad and commanded him to "Recite." He replied, "What shall I recite?" The result of his encounter with Gabriel is the Qur-an (the word itself means "recitation"), the holiest book in Islam. The Quranic revelations followed each other in brief intervals; at first, they were taught and learned by rote (still the custom in much of the Islamic world), but even during the prophet's lifetime, some verses were written down—on palm leaves, stones, indeed any available material. By the middle decades of the seventh century, during the caliphate of Omar and his successor Othman, an "authorized" version of the holy book was published. Middle Eastern Christianity was in a state of flux during the prophet's lifetime, with perhaps a majority of Arabian and Syrian Christians professing some form of the so-called Monophysite heresy. This doctrine held (contrary to the "two natures" doctrine of the council of Chalcedon) that after the incarnation, there was but a single, divine nature in the person of the incarnate Christ. Because the heresy centered on the transmutation of natures at the time of the birth of Jesus, the nativity and infancy tradition played an especially important role in the popular spread of Monophysite teaching. Hence, it is not surprising that Muhammad came into contact with the legendary material and that elements of the infancy tradition were finally incorporated in the Qur-an.

# Bibliographical Note

The recent update of the New Testament apocrypha edited by J. K. Elliott (*The Apocryphal New Testament* [Oxford: Clarendon, 1993]) promises to replace the 1924 edition of apocryphal texts by M. R. James, described below. Elliott's work also includes bibliographical references to critical editions available since the appearance of Wilson's 1963 translation of Hennecke-Schneemelcher's *New Testament Apocrypha*.

Indispensable to any consideration of the apocryphal tradition is Helmut Koester's recent study, *Ancient Christian Gospels, Their History and Significance* (London: SCM, 1990), which gives a full account of the early infancy narratives and of the "prevailing prejudices" concerning the distinction between canonical and apocryphal gospels.

The following are recommended for those who wish to pursue the study of the apocryphal infancy tradition.

- Collected texts in: Constantin Tischendorf, *Evangelia Apocrypha* (Leipzig, 1853; 2d ed., 1876); R. A. Lipsius, M. Bonnet, *Acta Apostolorum Apocrypha* (Leipzig, 1891–1903), German trans. by E. Hennecke and W. Schneemelcher, *Neutestamentliche Apokryphen* (NTA) (Tübingen, 1959). English readers will find reliable, if overly selective in its use of fragments and "extracts," the two-volume Hennecke-Schneemelcher, trans. by R. McL. Wilson (Philadelphia, 1963), and M. R. James, *The Apocryphal New Testament* (Oxford, 1924). The James translations suffer especially from the compiler's contrived Jacobean style as well as from an inordinate degree of abbreviation. Complete bibliography of studies (through 196) provided by James Charlesworth and J. Mueller, eds., *The New Testament Apocrypha and Pseudepigrapha: A Guide to Publications with Excursuses on Apocalypses* (Metuchen, N.J., and London: Scarecrow Press, 1987). Excludes studies of gnostic gospels except the *Gospel of Thomas*.

- On the *Book of James*: Greek text in Tischendorf, pp. 1–50. Commentaries: E. Amman, *Le Preévangile de Jacques et ses remaniements latins* (Paris, 1910); H. R. Smid, *Protevangelium Jacobi. A Commentary* (Assen, 1965); Oscar Cullmann in Hennecke-Schneemelcher I:277–90.

- On the infancy *Gospel of Thomas*: Greek text and Latin version in Tischendorf, pp. 140–80; Syriac text with English trans. by W. Wright, *Contributions to the Apocryphal Literature of the New Testament* (London, 1864), pp. 1–16; study by M. R. James, "The Gospel of Thomas," *Journal of Theological Studies* 30 (1929): 51–54; full bibliographical discussion by Cullmann in Hennecke-Schneemelcher, ET (English translation) I:388–89.

- On the fourth-century History of Joseph the Carpenter, C. Michel and P. Peeters, *Évangiles apocryphes*, I (Paris, 1924), in *Textes et documents pour l'étude historique du Christian-isme.*

- On the *Liber de infantia* or *Gospel of Pseudo-Matthew*, extracts and analysis in M. R. James, *Apocryphal New Testament*, pp. 71–79 (includes the forged epistles to and from St. Jerome, 70–72), text in Tischendorf, pp. 51–112 (who uses four manuscript versions). The book is an amplified version of the *Book of James* in chs. 1–17; chs. 18–24 incorporate legends of the sojourn into Egypt; chs. 25–41 deal broadly with the material contained in *Thomas*, ending with a move to Capernaum and a feast in honor of Jesus having reached his majority (ch. 42). In a variant, shortened form, the gospel is known as the Story of the Birth of Mary, from which the story of the first marriage of Joseph (pronounced heretical) was excised; this variant version was incorporated in the Golden Legend of James de Voragine (1298) through which it enjoyed wide popularity.

- On the Arabic Gospel of the Infancy, E. A. Wallis Budge, *Coptic Apocrypha* (London, 1899). The first ed. of the Arabic infancy gospel was printed in 1697 by Sike; reprinted in Tischendorf in Latin, pp. 181–209. Bibliographical discussion and extracts by Cullmann in Hennecke-Schneemelcher, I:404–17.

- On the Armenian Infancy Gospel, heavily dependent on the *Book of James*, critical ed. by Isaias D'Aiseti (Venice, 1898); C. Michel and P. Peeters, *Evangiles apocryphes*, II (Paris, 1914), including Syriac, Arabic, and Armenian infancy gospels.

- On the gnostic *Pistis Sophia*, Coptic text by C. Schmidt (Copenhagen, 1925); discussion by F. C. Burkitt, "Pistis Sophia," *Jour-*

*nal of Theological Studies* 23 (1921–22): 271–80; and Cullmann on its relation to the infancy stories in Hennecke-
Schneemelcher, I:401ff. (who terms it "gnostic legend").

- On the origin of the "Hymn of the Pearl," see especially
  A. F. J. Klijn, "The So-Called Hymn of the Pearl, ATh
  108–113," *Vigiliae Christianae* 14 (1960): 154–164, and
  Gunther Bornkamm's discussion in Hennecke-Schnee-
  melcher, ET, II:426–42; Hymn text, pp. 498–504 (from the
  Syriac.)

- On the Assumption of the Virgin, texts in Tischendorf, *Apocalypses Apocryphae* (Leipzig, 1866); Cullmann in NTA, I:429.

- On Gnosticism, including older surveys and contemporary
  appraisals, see Kurt Rudolph, *Gnosis* (Edinburgh, 1983), and
  Hans Jonas, *The Gnostic Religion* (Boston, 1958); texts from
  Nag Hammadi in *The Gnostic Scriptures,* translated and an-
  notated by Bentley Layton (London: SCM, 1987).

- On the so-called *Secret Gospel of Mark* discovered by Morton
  Smith, see his *Clement of Alexandria and a Secret Gospel of
  Mark* (Cambridge, Mass.: Harvard University Press, 1973).